Grain-Free Baking Made Simple

GRAIN-FREE BAKING
made simple

A COOKBOOK OF SWEET AND SAVORY RECIPES

JESSICA KIRK
Photography by Laura Flippen

ROCKRIDGE
PRESS

For general information on our other products and services or to obtain technical support, please contact our Customer Care Department within the United States at (866) 744-2665, or outside the United States at (510) 253-0500.

Rockridge Press publishes its books in a variety of electronic and print formats. Some content that appears in print may not be available in electronic books, and vice versa.

Interior and Cover Designer: Sean Doyle
Art Producer: Samantha Ulban
Editor: Van Van Cleave
Production Manager: Jose Olivera

Photography © 2022 Laura Flippen. Food styling by Laura Flippen. Author photo courtesy of Jess Kirk.
Cover Recipe: Sweet Cherry Galette

Paperback ISBN: 978-1-63878-700-6
eBook ISBN: 978-1-63878-528-6
R0

*This book is dedicated to my **father**,
who taught me that life is good,
and to my **mother**, who taught me to
simply trust in Him.*

Contents

Introduction

Hi, friend! I'm Jess and I'm so glad you're here. If we were meeting in person, I'd ask you to come on into my Southern kitchen and have a seat. Then, of course, I'd offer you something to eat that's warm and fluffy, baked right from my oven. But since we can't do that, I'm going to share my story and give you a glimpse into my grain-free kitchen from afar.

As a little girl, I remember being curled up into a little ball, rolling around on the floor in terrible pain. I had breathtaking stomachaches after eating almost anything, and I would become dehydrated from vomiting. I struggled to keep food down and was severely underweight. My childhood contained many hospital trips, doctor appointments, and misdiagnoses. At the time, no one could pinpoint what was going on. Then, during one emergency room visit in my early twenties, the doctor decided to test me for something I had never heard of before: celiac disease. Sure enough, I finally found the culprit that was making me sick.

I was instructed to change my diet and to start a new lifestyle. It was challenging. During that time, I found myself craving the foods I used to take for granted, especially all those soft, fluffy, doughy baked goods. At the time, I found next to nothing reliable or tasty to eat for those of us leading a gluten-free or grain-free lifestyle. So, I started researching what I could and couldn't eat, and I created my own recipes from scratch.

I've spent the past decade working to craft delicious, satisfying recipes that you could never tell were grain-free. After many family members, friends, neighbors, and colleagues continuously asked me to share my recipes, I decided to start a website, BlessHerHeartYall.com. It helped many people around the world enjoy the baked goods they loved while maintaining their health. Grain-free recipes help not only those with celiac disease but also those with a grain allergy or sensitivity, and even loved ones who cook and bake for those who choose to lead a grain-free lifestyle. I met many wonderful people who were going through the same thing as I did. Finally, I felt like I wasn't alone in my struggle to maintain a grain-free life.

I've been on a gluten-free diet for 12 years now and have converted many of my former favorite recipes into grain-free versions. Every year it becomes easier and faster to enjoy the comforts of home cooking in grain-free form. I know the difficulties of adopting and maintaining a grain-free diet, and I will share what I've learned with you in this book. Friend, you are not alone on this journey. I'm here to encourage you and walk you through some of the lessons I had to learn the hard way all those years ago.

This cookbook is a much-needed resource for grain-free baked goods that don't require a lot of time, effort, expertise, or money. Whether you're a seasoned baker or just starting out, this book is for you. You will find delicious baked recipes, stories of my experiences along the way, and a mix of helpful tips for using grain-free ingredients at home. Now, go preheat the oven, grab that apron, and let's get baking.

CHAPTER ONE

AGAINST THE GRAIN

It can be more than a bit overwhelming when you first begin baking grain-free. In this section, I'll walk you through what you'll need to know before you start baking (including how I'm defining "grain-free"), some of the benefits of a grain-free lifestyle, and tips for setting up your kitchen. I'll also answer some frequently asked questions about the grain-free diet. Your all-in-one guide to grain-free baking awaits!

Defining Grain-Free

Before we jump into the recipes for delicious grain-free baked goods, I'd like to explain what I mean by "grain-free" since there are many different versions of grain-free diets.

My definition of a grain-free diet is one that is free from all grains, including corn, wheat, rice, barley, rye, oat, spelt, millet, and sorghum, and all products derived from these ingredients. Ingredients like corn syrup and rice cakes should also be eliminated from the diet in order to keep your foods truly grain-free. I'd also like to note that foods that are very similar to grains, like quinoa, can still be eaten in a grain-free diet since they are not actually grains, but more like pseudo-cereals.

Many times, someone starting out on a grain-free journey will also need to exclude dairy from their diets. This may be because of allergies or intolerances, for weight loss, or simply to adopt a healthier lifestyle. No matter the reasoning, many of us need grain-free recipes that also eliminate other foods. Throughout this book, I've included tips on how to make these grain-free recipes sugar-free and dairy-free as well.

Eliminating Grains

Eliminating grains can be beneficial for many people, not just those with allergies or intolerances to one or more grains. Some people go grain-free in order to lose weight, while others might want to try to balance their gut microbiome. No matter what your reason is to move to a grain-free diet, you've come to the right place.

When adopting a new diet, the first step is always the hardest. In this case, I suggest beginning with a deep cleanse of your kitchen pantry and refrigerator to remove all the items that include grains. I also recommend removing products that have been processed in facilities where grains have also been handled. Don't forget about common grain "traps" or foods that you wouldn't think would have grains in them, such as premade sauces and salad dressings. These processed foods may include ingredients like corn syrup or may have been cross-contaminated during the manufacturing process. Also, be diligent in checking the ingredients of any spice blends or premade meal kits.

Lastly, you will likely need to throw away any pasta, noodles, cereal, baking mixes, and even certain drinks. If you need to keep these items for someone else in your household, label them clearly so you don't accidentally use them when you mean to use your grain-free ingredients.

Better Baking Bases

When we think of baking, often the first ingredient we think of is flour. Many flours are derived from grains, so the first challenge in building your grain-free pantry will be stocking grain-free flours. However, grain-free and gluten-free flours can often yield destabilized bakes, resulting in some less-than-desirable final baked goods. Cakes may have crumbly textures, pastries may fall apart, and breads might not rise. Whatever the case, it's a sad day when your baked goods don't live up to their potential. Fortunately, if you use the proper flour blends correctly, I promise no sacrifices will be made to texture or taste.

In this book, I will be sharing my special flour blends with you all so you can have the best possible grain-free bakes. The first flour blend is a great all-purpose, grain-free blend used for many of this book's sweet recipes. I've also created a delicious savory version that I use for many of the recipes in chapter 9. Lastly, I use a great grain-free biscuit mix to keep certain breads and other baked goods light and perfectly fluffy.

Healthier Baking

It's worth noting that there is a difference in the nutritional value between standard baking and grain-free baking. I've compiled a list of some of the potential differences between the two baking types. Additionally, in the subsequent sections, I discuss a few of the other dietary considerations when eating dairy-free and sugar-free.

The most notable nutritional advantage of grains is that they are a good source of fiber. Fiber contributes to many functions of the body, including making you feel full and satiated as well as keeping your digestive tract running smoothly. Many people worry that a grain-free diet may be a drastic change for the body, leading to constipation or satiety issues.

However, you can still get plenty of fiber in your diet from other foods, like dark-green veggies, fruits, nuts, and beans. If you eat a well-balanced diet, watch your intake of vitamins and minerals, and talk to your doctor about your diet choices, a grain-free diet should not affect your health in a negative way.

Additionally, grain-free diets can offer sufferers potential relief from a multitude of symptoms that result from grain intolerances, including headaches and brain fog, fatigue, stomach pains and bloat, diarrhea and constipation, and eczema. Individuals may also experience lowered blood pressure levels, reduced inflammation, and improved mental health.

Before you make any major dietary changes, be sure to talk to your doctor to decide if going grain-free is the right choice for you.

Dairy-Free

Some individuals give up both grains and dairy in pursuit of eating healthier and feeling better. Others, like myself, may experience intolerances to both. In this book, there are a number of recipes that are totally dairy-free, such as my Gooey-Center Naan Bread (page 24), Banana Split Cupcakes (page 50), and Blackberry Crumble (page 87). These recipes will be noted with a dairy-free label. Other recipes may include dairy products in their ingredients, but whenever this is the case, I will always provide dairy-free substitution options.

Please be mindful that in making substitutions or changes to the recipes, there may be changes in the final product's taste, texture, look, or density. Use substitutions carefully to ensure the best baked goods. Whenever possible, I'll give you tips on specific products to use that produce the best results when substituting dairy-free ingredients.

Refined Sugar—Free

Some bakers give up both grains and refined sugar in pursuit of eating healthier and feeling better, too. There are a number of recipes in this book that are totally free of refined sugar, such as my Peanut Butter Cookies (page 39), Sandwich Bread (page 28), Dark Chocolate Cupcakes (page 51), and Coffee Cake Cupcakes (page 48). These recipes will have a sugar-free label. Other recipes call for sugar, but they also include a substitution option for a natural sweetener, such as honey, pure maple syrup, or monk fruit or coconut sugars.

I am picky about the products that I use in my kitchen. My favorite go-to coconut sugar is **Big Tree Farms Organic Brown Coconut Sugar**, which acts very similarly to light brown sugar in my experience. It is a light golden brown, which helps gives baked goods a golden hue, and it is lightly sticky, just like light brown sugar, so it doesn't clump into hard balls like many other coconut sugars tend to do.

In this book, I use two different monk fruit sugar varieties: monk fruit baking sugar, which acts like a granulated white sugar in baked goods, and a monk fruit powdered sugar, which acts and tastes just like regular powdered sugar. My favorite monk fruit baking sugar to use is the **Monk Fruit In The Raw** brand sweetener. My favorite monk fruit powdered sugar is the **Lakanto Sugar-Free Powdered Monk Fruit Sweetener**.

Grain-Free Baking FAQs

It's completely normal to have questions when you're beginning a new dietary journey. To make things easier for you, I've listed some of the more commonly asked questions I receive about the grain-free lifestyle here. If you have any additional concerns, you should reach out to a medical professional or dietitian for personalized guidance.

Will I miss out on important nutrition with a grain-free diet?

Absolutely not. Grain-free foods do not have grains, but they do keep the rest of the nutritional benefits of the dish. Remember, the only thing different about going grain-free is removing the grain from your diet, nothing more.

Will my energy level fluctuate more while eating a grain-free diet?

I've never felt tired or sluggish because of my grain-free diet, and I have not heard a complaint about this from others in the plethora of grain-free groups I am a part of. In fact, brain fog tends to go away when you adopt a grain-free diet, and I definitely have more energy while following a grain-free diet. Many grain-free friends and readers have felt the same.

Can I still enjoy the foods that I love?

You sure can. I still eat all my favorite foods—they are just homemade (and frankly, they taste better!). In this book, I've compiled a collection of easy-to-make and commonly asked-for baked goods, such as bread, pizza, doughnuts, and even sugar cookies.

Where can I shop for grain-free products?

You can find grain-free products anywhere and everywhere you shop for regular foods. Most larger chain grocery stores, specialty and health food grocers, as well as online retailers, including Amazon, stock large selections of grain-free products.

Is grain-free cooking more expensive?

It may be a bit more expensive at first when stocking up on the grain-free essentials that you need to kick-start your grain-free journey. After that, you'll likely not even notice a difference to your grocery bill.

Will I still feel satisfied and full after eating a grain-free recipe?

Yes, you will feel both satisfied and satiated. Grain-free foods remove the grains, not the nutrients, and can be just as tasty!

Should I worry about cross-contamination?

Yes, you definitely should. Most manufactured products give information on their website about the possibility of products being cross-contaminated. If you are worried about cross-contamination, then look for food products that are certified grain-free, as these are far less likely to be contaminated.

Does it get easier to eat and bake grain-free after a while?

Yes, it sure does! When you first start eating grain-free, it can feel overwhelming and daunting. In time, reading ingredient lists and preparing your foods becomes much easier. You just need to allow yourself the time to learn and adjust to your new grain-free normal.

Will I lose weight on a grain-free diet?

I can only speak on my own behalf on this one. I have been able to maintain my current weight for years on my grain-free diet. I've heard that some people do lose weight, while I've heard the opposite from others. I'd recommend talking with your doctor about whether a grain-free diet is right for you and your current weight status and goals.

Now that we've discussed what eating grain-free may look like for you, let's move on to preparing and stocking your grain-free kitchen in chapter 2.

Pizza Crust, 30

GRAIN-FREE BAKER'S KITCHEN

I wouldn't be doing you any justice if I didn't dive into grain-free kitchens before we start our grain-free baking journey. This chapter will discuss prepping your kitchen and your ingredients for the best baking outcomes. It will teach you how to properly measure all your baking ingredients, how to organize your kitchen to make things easier for you while baking, and what equipment you should consider having in your home. I will also explain how to turn a few common fails into fixes and even share my favorite homemade and store-bought flour blends. I'll cover everything you need in order to get started baking grain-free.

Cleanse the Space

The first step to going grain-free begins with a deep cleanse of your kitchen counters and a purge of your food pantry and refrigerator to remove all the items that have grain in them. Don't forget about those common grain "traps" that were discussed in chapter 1 (page 2).

You should remove or separate grains from your grain-free ingredients, and you should also deep clean your kitchen after cooking with grains to ensure that there is no cross-contamination during the grain-free baking process. Make sure to use household, kitchen-safe cleaners on your kitchen countertops and inside small appliances such as your microwave and your stand mixer. Also be sure to check for any crumbs or residue resting in the folds of your kitchen towel or other tools.

Lastly, don't forget to clean the handles, buttons, and doors that you touch without even thinking about it. Grains can be sneaky, and we don't want to unintentionally ingest grain when it could be prevented in the first place.

Equipment Made Simple

The pieces of equipment listed below are what you will need to have on hand in order to create the recipes in this book. For each item listed, I've included a brief description of why it is so important for you to have in your kitchen. You may already have some of these items at home, such as measuring cups or a hand mixer.

Handheld Electric Mixer

Use this tool for whisking wet ingredients, batters, and doughs much faster than you can do by hand. Hand mixers are also typically smaller and lighter than their cousin, the stand mixer.

Stand Mixer

This tool does the same job as the handheld mixer but it does so with a heavy-duty capacity. Thick bread doughs and sticky, thick batters don't stand a chance against this powerful kitchen appliance.

Precise Liquid Measuring Cup

When used the right way, a liquid measuring cup allows you to accurately determine the right amount of liquid for your bakes. And what is the correct way to use liquid measuring cups? Glad you asked! Carefully pour the liquid into the bottom of the measuring cup up to the desired line demarcated, ensuring that the lowest level of liquid (the bottom of the meniscus, if present) is at the desired measure line. Check out the Mastering Measurements section on page 20 for more details.

Heavy-Duty Apron

When you work with so many different ingredients, spills are inevitable. Protect your clothing by wearing an apron. A heavy-duty one will last you through many washes and many kitchen adventures.

Mixing Bowls

A set of stainless-steel mixing bowls with small, medium, and large options is perfect for your kitchen. I like working with stainless-steel bowls because it is easy to feel the temperature of the ingredients with your hands. They are also a breeze to clean and are dishwasher-safe.

Recipe Book Holder

There's nothing more annoying than your cookbook flipping shut when you have your hands all floured up, causing you to lose your page. I highly recommend getting your hands on a cookbook holder that will keep your book open for you.

PAN OF THE MOMENT

You may notice that throughout this book, I call for different sizes, shapes, and materials for baking pans in my recipes. There is a method to my madness. Different sizes and shapes cook differently and different materials produce varying results.

THE LOAF PAN For most of my breads, a loaf pan is used, whether it is made of glass or aluminum foil. The shape of the loaf pan gives bread its preferred bread shape as well as the perfect surface area in order for the dough to rise and form into billowy, soft slices of bread.

THE SQUARE PAN The 8-inch square pan is perfect for bars, as it helps stabilize the treats in a compact form.

THE BAKING SHEET A 13-by-18-inch nonstick rimmed baking sheet will also never go out of style, baking things like cookies evenly and stopping overflows and spills before they could ever happen. The nonstick feature also makes cleanup a breeze.

6-RING NONSTICK DOUGHNUT PAN These simple pans turn batters into perfect rings. Even though these pans are nonstick, I still recommend that you grease or use cooking spray on the pan before introducing the batter into each of the 6 forms.

MUFFIN TINS I highly recommend owning a standard 12-count muffin tin and 24-count mini muffin tin because most recipes make enough batter to create at least that many muffins, if not more. I also recommend purchasing nonstick tins so your baked treats come out easily.

PIE PLATE When referring to a pie plate within the pages of this book, I am referring to a glass or ceramic 9-inch pie plate. I have found throughout the years that using a glass or ceramic pie plate over a metal one creates a more uniform baked crust, the base for all pies.

RAMEKINS Ramekins are used multiple times throughout this book. I gravitate toward the basic 4-ounce round white ramekins made of porcelain. There are other sizes and materials out there, but all the recipes that use the 4-ounce porcelain ramekins in my kitchen come out perfectly.

FAILS YOU CAN FIX

You can't bake grain-free without a fail or two. Fortunately for us, many fails can be fixed. Below I've listed a few common grain-free baking fails alongside their solutions.

TEXTURE IS WAY OFF Maybe you've heard the terms *gritty*, *crumbly*, *dense*, or *hard* to describe grain-free baked goods. Or maybe even the opposite: *chunky*, *mushy*, or *gummy*. It's notoriously tricky to get the right texture in grain-free foods because the gluten—that special protein that holds things together and makes them soft and fluffy—has been removed. I will share tips that I've learned that will fix this texture problem for good.

LACK OF RISE Gluten is responsible for the rise in common baked goods, which is why so many gluten-free and grain-free baked goods end up flat and dense. However, by using a combination of the right flours, starches, and blends, you'll be able to create light and fluffy grain-free baked goods in your own kitchen.

TOO MUCH SPREAD Another common problem with grain-free baking is with cookies and crackers that spread out too far. This can produce thin, crispy, hard, and sometimes burned baked goods. The gluten that is lacking in these recipes was there to bind and stick the cracker or cookie together. I'll show you how to replace that gluten with a grain-free binder.

OVERBAKED Sometimes in mid-bake you realize that your creation is turning really dark brown and it's not even close to the time to take it out of the oven. There are a couple things that you can do. First off, make sure that your time is correct and that the oven is set at the correct temperature, a big mistake that I have made many times over. If all your settings are correct, I suggest grabbing a large piece of aluminum foil and covering your bake to help prevent any further browning of the top. The heat from the oven will still allow the insides of your goodies to bake, but the browning of the top will slow.

UNDERCOOKED There are also those times where your baked good comes out of the oven too soft, too mushy, or too gummy. Now what? I like to add more heat. Typically, I will place my item back into the oven to cook longer. If that is not an option, I like to toast my baked good to crisp it up quickly. You'd be surprised what a few extra minutes of heat can do to your baked goods.

Homemade Grain-Free Flour Blends

Homemade grain-free flour blends will be your best friend when baking your grain-free goods. Below you will find three of my go-to flour blends and mixes based on the type of baked good I'm creating. When it comes to these blends, I prefer to make my own, because homemade blends are much more affordable than store-bought varieties. You will also get a higher yield out of one batch of homemade grain-free flour blend than you typically get from a single bag of store-bought grain-free flour blend. Fortunately, all the ingredients for my blends can be purchased from big-box grocers, and it only takes a minute or two to mix them together. These blends, when stored correctly, can last for months, so don't ignore the storage instructions.

Sweet Grain-Free Flour Blend

Prep Time: 2 minutes

Use this flour blend when making sweet dishes that call for all-purpose flour. This grain-free substitute yields the best texture when you're trying to match that of regular all-purpose flour blends when baking sweet treats. Please also note that tapioca flour can sometimes be labeled as tapioca starch.

Makes **4 cups**

1½ cups almond flour
1 cup cassava flour
½ cup coconut flour
½ cup chickpea flour
½ cup tapioca flour

Mix the almond flour, cassava flour, coconut flour, chickpea flour, and tapioca flour together in a large mixing bowl until well combined. Store in a food-safe storage container or plastic bag at room temperature for up to 2 months.

Substitutions: You can replace the tapioca flour or tapioca starch with potato starch for a slightly different taste profile and consistency.

Savory Grain-Free Flour Blend

Prep Time: 2 minutes

Use this flour blend when making savory dishes that call for all-purpose flour. This grain-free substitute has the best texture for matching regular all-purpose flour blends, without adding any ingredients that would add a sweet taste to the blend. Please note that tapioca flour can sometimes be labeled as tapioca starch.

Makes **4 cups**

2 cups almond flour
1 cup cassava flour
½ cup chickpea flour
½ cup tapioca flour

Mix the almond flour, cassava flour, chickpea flour, and tapioca flour together in a large mixing bowl until well combined. Store in a food-safe storage container or plastic bag at room temperature for up to 2 months.

Substitutions: You can replace the tapioca flour or tapioca starch with potato starch for a slightly different taste profile and consistency.

Grain-Free Biscuit Mix

Prep Time: 2 minutes

When I want to create a baked good and have it turn out nice and fluffy and airy, I will always use this biscuit mix. It is great to use in breads, rolls, biscuits of all kinds, and muffins that you want to be light. You can keep this recipe dairy-free by substituting dry coconut milk powder for the milk powder. Part of the purpose of this powder is to add a touch of sweet.

Makes 5¼ cups

2 cups chickpea flour
1¼ cups coconut flour
1 cup dry milk powder
½ cup coconut sugar
½ cup arrowroot flour
1 tablespoon baking
   powder
1 teaspoon baking soda
½ teaspoon salt

Mix the chickpea flour, coconut flour, milk powder, coconut sugar, arrowroot flour, baking powder, baking soda, and salt together in a large mixing bowl until well combined. Store in a food-safe storage container or plastic bag at room temperature for up to 2 months.

Substitutions: You can substitute monk fruit baking sugar for the coconut sugar and dry coconut milk powder for the dry milk powder. These substitutions can provide not only a sugar-free and dairy-free option but also a slightly different taste profile and consistency.

Ready-Made Flour Brands

Though I prefer to use homemade grain-free flour and biscuit blends in my baked recipes, I understand the obvious convenience of buying ready-made, resealable, grain-free flour blends. They truly make baking as simple as possible. I've tried numerous name brands over the years, and I've listed my favorites here in order of my preference.

My top store-bought grain-free flour blend is from the King Arthur line of baking products. **King Arthur Grain-Free Paleo Baking Flour** creates the most consistent baked goods. The biggest downside is that it's more expensive. A more accessible grain-free flour option is **Bob's Red Mill Grain-Free Paleo Baking Flour**. It's more affordable and still produces a nicely textured baked good. If you don't have the time to make your own grain-free flour blend, grab a bag of one of these two products. While they won't save you money, the additional time you'll save may be beneficial in certain situations.

Quick Tips for Baking Grain-Free

The recipes in this book are easy, but there are still some general best practices to keep in mind while baking grain-free. I've included them here so you can spend less time fixing things and more time enjoying your perfect baked goods.

Read the Entire Recipe before Baking

Whoops! You're halfway through baking a cake for the party tonight and just noticed a component that needs to chill overnight. Reading the entire recipe before you start baking will help you avoid sticky situations like this one in addition to familiarizing you with the ingredients and techniques. In fact, I have made a rule in my own kitchen: read twice, bake once.

Read Those Labels

Many grocery stores and online retailers have labels or guides for products that are grain-free. Usually, the front label will advertise that the ingredient is a grain-free product as a key selling point. However, sometimes you must dig through the ingredient list on the back of the nutrition label in order to figure out if the product is truly grain-free or not. Be meticulous and read those food labels carefully.

Room-Temperature Ingredients

Another incredibly important factor when baking is the temperature of your ingredients. If a recipe calls for a room-temperature egg, there is good reasoning behind it. You'd be surprised at how many times I put a cold egg into a batter that called for a room-temperature egg, and the final baked good did not turn out as predicted. If a recipe describes the butter as needing to be softened, make sure that your butter has had time to warm up before incorporating it into your recipe. Every ingredient works differently at different temperatures, so pay close attention to the temperature details in a recipe, and don't chance it with ingredients that are too warm or cold.

Shaping the Dough First

Many doughs will need to be preshaped, allowed to rise, and then shaped again. Don't skip the preshape step! Preshaping dough is important because it helps create a more uniform texture with appropriately sized air holes, giving your breads that even lightness we all love. Shaping also helps create surface tension, which holds your bread together; encourages it to rise in the oven; and yields a smooth, even, crispy crust.

The most popular way to shape your dough is into a ball. To do so, lightly flour your hands and your flat work surface. Roll your dough into one large ball with both hands, tucking the sides of the dough ball underneath itself until you form a smooth, tight ball. Then, let your dough rest for 10 to 40 minutes—otherwise known as the "bench rest." This helps relax the dough, so the final shaping stage is easier and faster for you.

When you're ready for the final shaping, typically you will repeat the steps you took for the preshaping. Be sure to take note of the consistency of your dough at this stage. If it's on the wet side or is sticking to your hands while touching it, you will need to move fast during the final shaping. If you find that your rested dough is more on the dry side, more movement and shaping will be needed to relax it.

Oven Temperature Tips

I had a terrible habit for many, many years of throwing any dough or batter into the oven as soon as it was ready, whether the oven was up to temperature or not. What could go wrong? Trust me—a lot can go wrong. Don't make my mistake; give the oven those few extra minutes to heat up to full temperature before sliding your unbaked goods into the oven. I promise that fiddling with a half-baked, burned, or unrisen good that was baked at too low of a temperature will cost you more time and energy in the long run. Always put your concoction in the oven when the oven is at the right temperature. Additionally, if the instructions direct you to lower the oven temperature while your baked good is in the oven, lower it to the exact temperature mentioned.

Using Your Measuring Cups Correctly

When we're baking, it's very tempting to drop our measuring cups into a big flour bag and then grab a whopping scoop to use in our recipes. Unfortunately, this method packs the flour together, meaning that you will actually be using more flour than the recipe requires. This will offset the correct ingredient ratios, resulting in denser baked goods. You will have much more success baking grain-free in your home if you scoop your dry ingredients into your measuring cup using a spoon. This will allow you to create the recipe as the original designer intended, and your baked goods are more likely to come out fluffy and risen. Always fight the urge to scoop your cups!

Prep like a Pro

It is extremely important to prepare your workspace to bake before you start in on a recipe. There are many ways home bakers can set themselves up for a successful baking session. Some of my favorite ways to prep for baking masterpieces include the following.

Mise en Place

This is one of my favorite ways to prep and makes the entire baking process so much faster and smoother. *Mise en place* is a French term that refers to when a chef or baker prepares their ingredients beforehand, including cleaning, cutting, dicing, chopping, mashing, and, of course, measuring each and every ingredient. That means all ingredients can be added easily to the recipe at the exact time they're needed, which makes for a more pleasant and less stressful baking experience.

Empty the Dishwasher and Sink

It is so helpful to start your baking process with an empty kitchen sink and an empty dishwasher. As you get further into your recipe, you can simply move the used dishes and kitchen gadgets you collect out of your way. The best system that I've found is to toss your dirty dishes into the sink or dishwasher as you go. You can't do that if your sink and dishwasher are already full.

Dedicate a Shelf or Cupboard

I have a dedicated cupboard in my kitchen in which I store all of my grain-free baking ingredients. I do this so that I am always going to the same place for ingredients and am less likely to misplace items I need in my recipes. I also recommend keeping this shelf or cupboard close to the oven or toward the center of your kitchen, if you can. This will save you time running back and forth to grab ingredients.

Read the Entire Recipe

I've mentioned it before, and I'll mention it again: Read your recipe before you start baking! Better yet, read the entire recipe twice through. By doing this, you'll catch things you need to know that you might've missed on the first read-through (and that you definitely would miss if you just read the recipe on the fly).

Mastering Measurements

I mention how important it is to measure ingredients correctly multiple times in this book, and for good reason. Correctly measuring ingredients takes a bit more effort and time on the front end but can drastically affect the final outcome. Baking does require a more exact measuring than cooking typically requires, but once you get used to this new technique, it will become second nature to you.

DRY INGREDIENTS

There is a definite difference between baking with properly measured dry ingredients and when you don't. To properly measure your dry ingredients, spoon the ingredient into your measuring cup until it reaches the top of the measuring cup in an even layer. Do not pour the dry ingredient into the measuring cup or scoop the measuring cup directly into the dry ingredient itself to fill it. Level off your measurements using the straight edge of a butter knife, then add them to your bowl.

WET INGREDIENTS

To accurately measure wet or liquid ingredients by volume, gently pour the wet ingredient into a liquid measuring cup until the bottom of the meniscus, the curve on the surface of the liquid, hits the desired demarcated line that represents the amount you need for your recipe.

Lastly, some wet ingredients with higher viscosities, such as honey or pure maple syrup, will be harder to measure than other wet ingredients, such as milk or water. I recommend measuring out these types of wet ingredients last due to the added work of scraping them out of your measuring cups.

About the Recipes

This book is designed to be a comprehensive, straightforward starting point for those looking to begin their grain-free journey. With that in mind, let me walk you through how to navigate the chapters to come. The recipe chapters will show you how to make breads, cookies and bars, pastries and muffins, cakes and cupcakes, pies and tarts, and savory bites. Inside each chapter, you'll find numerous delicious recipes broken down into specific ingredient lists and easy-to-follow instructions that will allow you to make the perfect baked good you desire. On top of those necessities, I have also included recipe tips and tricks with each recipe, such as variations of my favorite flavors, straightforward storage recommendations, and simple baking tips to make it even easier for you in your kitchen. Finally, because this book aims to serve the widest possible audience, I've added the following recipe labels to help you determine if any specific recipe is best for you:

- Dairy-free
- Egg-free
- Freezable
- Nut-free
- Refined sugar-free

Now you're ready to begin your grain-free baking adventure. I hope you enjoy these baked goods as much as I do and that your experience within this book's pages brings you both the comforts of home and the confidence to continue your grain-free journey.

CHAPTER THREE

BREADS AND FLATBREADS

For the novice grain-free baker, breads will usually seem the hardest and most daunting. Thankfully, I have put together a wide range of breads and flatbreads that are as easy to bake as they are to devour. These bread recipes create soft, doughy, and moist bread for you to enjoy with your family, slice by slice.

Gooey-Center Naan Bread

Egg-Free, Freezable, Nut-Free, Refined Sugar–Free
Prep Time: 20 minutes / Rise Time: 90 minutes / Chill Time: 15 minutes
Cook Time: 16 minutes

Naan bread was always one of the breads that I missed the most when going gluten- and grain-free. Each bite of this grain-free version has a golden baked crust and a soft, doughy, almost gooey center layer. Place the naan on a serving plate, wrapped in a clean kitchen towel, and let it sit in the microwave until ready to serve. This keeps your naan bread warm and soft until you're ready to eat it.

Makes **4 naan**

¾ cup warm water
   (115°F)
1 (0.25-ounce) package
   instant yeast
1 teaspoon honey
1½ cups cassava flour,
   plus more for dusting
½ cup tapioca flour
1 teaspoon baking
   powder
½ teaspoon salt
1 tablespoon olive oil,
   plus more for greasing
   and cooking
¼ cup plain yogurt
1 teaspoon apple cider
   vinegar

1. In a small bowl, combine the water, yeast, and honey. Let it sit for 5 to 10 minutes until fizzy on top.

2. In a stand mixer, mix the flours, baking powder, and salt. Add the yeast mixture and mix until combined.

3. Mix in the olive oil, yogurt, and vinegar until combined.

4. Using the dough hook attachment, knead the dough for 5 minutes.

5. Place the dough in an oiled bowl and cover with a clean kitchen towel. Place the bowl in a warm spot and allow the dough to rise for 90 minutes or until it's doubled in size.

6. Once the dough has risen, place it in the refrigerator to chill for 10 to 15 minutes.

7. Flour your hands and counter. Roll the dough into 4 or 5 equal-size balls. Place each ball between two sheets of wax paper, then roll each ball into a circle about 1/3 inch thick.

8. Drizzle a large nonstick pan with oil and heat over medium-high heat. Place each piece of dough on the heated pan one at a time and cook for 1 to 2 minutes per side or until the dough is a deep golden brown. The edges should also puff up.

9. Transfer the cooked naan to a cooling rack and enjoy.

Pro Tip: The thinner you roll out the dough, the less time it takes to cook. Thinner dough will also be crispier.

Crispy Sweet Cinnamon Flatbread

Dairy-Free, Refined Sugar–Free
Prep Time: 10 minutes / Chill Time: 30 minutes / Bake Time: 15 minutes

I am in love with this sweet version of flatbread. This soft baked bread is delicious. Cut it into squares or triangles and dip it into sweet dips like fruit dip or whipped cream, or top it with seasonal berries, honey, caramel, or chocolate chips. No matter how you choose to enjoy it, this bread is a treat for your sweet tooth.

Makes 4 flatbreads

2¼ cups almond flour
½ cup coconut sugar
1 teaspoon baking powder
1 teaspoon ground cinnamon
½ teaspoon fine sea salt
1 large egg
2 tablespoons pure maple syrup
2 tablespoons coconut oil

1. In a large mixing bowl, combine the flour, sugar, baking powder, cinnamon, and salt and mix well.

2. Add the egg, maple syrup, and oil and stir until well combined. Place the bowl in the refrigerator for 30 minutes to chill.

3. Preheat the oven to 325°F.

4. Lay out a sheet of parchment paper on your work surface. Divide the chilled dough into 4 equal parts. Place the dough on the paper. Cover the dough with a second sheet of parchment paper that's the same size. Roll the 4 pieces of dough with a rolling pin into rectangles that are ⅛ to ¼ inch thick. Transfer the parchment and dough rectangles to a large baking sheet. Carefully peel off the top sheet of parchment.

5. Bake for 13 to 15 minutes or until the edges turn golden but the centers are still soft. Allow to cool and harden for a few minutes on the baking sheet before moving them to a cooling rack.

Variation Tip: You can easily substitute honey for the maple syrup with a 1:1 ratio.

Pumpkin Bread

Freezable
Prep Time: 10 minutes / **Bake Time:** 55 minutes

Nothing screams fall more than the flavor of pumpkin. This pumpkin bread has a lovely amount of spice and mellow sweetness. The gentle flavors of this bread make it perfect as the main treat for breakfast or brunch or as a sweet side dish for dinner.

Serves 12

Nonstick cooking spray
2 tablespoons unsalted
   butter, softened
½ cup granulated sugar
½ cup light brown
   coconut sugar
2 large eggs, room
   temperature
½ (15-ounce) can
   pumpkin puree
1½ cups Grain-Free
   Biscuit Mix (page 16)
1 teaspoon ground
   cinnamon
½ teaspoon pumpkin
   spice
¼ teaspoon ground
   cloves

1. Preheat the oven to 350°F, then spray a 9" x 5" 1-pound loaf pan with cooking spray. Set aside.

2. In a large mixing bowl, combine the butter, sugars, eggs, and pumpkin puree, then mix until smooth. Add the biscuit mix, cinnamon, pumpkin spice, and cloves. Mix again until well combined and smooth.

3. Pour the batter into the prepared loaf pan and bake on the middle rack for 50 to 55 minutes or until the top and edges of the loaf are golden brown. A toothpick inserted into the center of the loaf should come out clean when its fully baked.

4. Allow the bread to cool to room temperature before slicing and serving.

Ingredient Tip: Double-check to make sure that the can of pumpkin you're using for this recipe is pureed pumpkin and not pumpkin pie filling. The latter will not work here and your recipe will not turn out correctly. Plus, it has extra sugar and other additives.

Sandwich Bread

Dairy-Free, Freezable, Refined Sugar–Free
Prep Time: 20 minutes / Rise Time: 1 hour / Bake Time: 40 minutes

This recipe yields soft, moist slices of classic bread. They're perfect for scrumptious sandwiches or as breakfast toast smothered with melted butter and jam. As the loaf is used, the last few slices are great to cube into homemade croutons.

Serves 12

Nonstick cooking spray
1 (0.25-ounce) package instant yeast
¾ cup warm water (about 115°F)
3 large egg whites
¼ cup olive oil
1½ tablespoons apple cider vinegar
¼ cup light brown coconut sugar
3 cups Savory Grain-Free Flour Blend (page 15)
2¼ teaspoons xanthan gum
½ teaspoon baking powder

1. Spray a 9-by-5-inch glass loaf pan with cooking spray and set aside. In a small bowl, combine the yeast and warm water. Set aside.

2. In a stand mixer with the whisk attachment, beat the egg whites at medium-high speed for 5 to 7 minutes, until stiff peaks form.

3. Add the olive oil and vinegar to the yeast mixture, then slowly pour it into the bowl with the stiffened egg whites while your mixer is on medium speed. Add the coconut sugar, flour blend, xanthan gum, and baking powder. Continue mixing on medium speed until a smooth dough forms.

4. Place the dough in the greased loaf pan and cover with a clean kitchen towel. Allow the dough to rise for 1 hour in a warm location. Preheat the oven to 350°F.

5. Bake the dough on the middle rack for 35 to 40 minutes. Allow the bread to cool in the pan for 2 to 3 minutes before transferring it to a cooling rack to cool completely before serving.

Pro Tip: Homemade bread needs to be eaten pretty quickly since it doesn't contain the preservatives present in store-bought breads. Make this recipe when you have 3 to 4 days to devour it.

Classic Flatbread

Freezable, Refined Sugar–Free
Prep Time: 15 minutes / Bake Time: 11 minutes

Many grain-free flatbreads become soggy when sauce or cheeses are added to them. Not the case for this classic flatbread! Whether you like a Margherita-style flatbread or find yourself dreaming of barbecue chicken or sundried tomato and pesto, this flatbread recipe can handle it all.

Serves 4

Nonstick cooking spray
1¾ cups Savory Grain-Free Flour Blend (page 15)
½ teaspoon salt
½ teaspoon xanthan gum
1 (0.25-ounce) package instant yeast
½ cup warm milk (around 115°F)
3 tablespoons unsalted butter, softened
1 large egg, room temperature
1 tablespoon honey
½ teaspoon apple cider vinegar
Toppings, as desired

1. Preheat the oven to 450°F. Spray a large nonstick baking sheet with cooking spray. Set aside.

2. In the bowl of a stand mixer, combine the flour blend, salt, and xanthan gum.

3. Make a small hole with your finger in the middle of the flour mixture and pour the yeast into that hole. Pour the warm milk over the yeast.

4. Add the butter, egg, honey, and vinegar. Using the dough hook attachment, mix until fully combined, about 2 minutes.

5. Spray your hands with cooking spray and place the dough on the prepared baking sheet, then flatten it into a large rectangle about ½ inch thick.

6. Bake on the middle rack for 6 minutes. Remove the flatbread from the oven and add the toppings you'd like. Bake again for about 5 minutes or until it reaches your desired crispness.

Pro Tip: For a cheesy pesto flatbread, sprinkle 1 cup diced vegetables on top of the dough, then drizzle with ¼ cup gluten-free pesto and top with 2 cups shredded mozzarella cheese. Place the flatbread back in the oven for 4 to 5 minutes or until the cheese has melted and turned golden brown around the edges.

Pizza Crust

Freezable, Refined Sugar–Free
Prep Time: 15 minutes / **Bake Time:** 10 minutes

One of almost everyone's first cravings when going grain-free is pizza. This pizza crust recipe is perfect for one larger pizza or a few smaller, personal-size pizzas. It's delicious with marinara sauce, white sauce, or olive oil–based pizza sauces, and it can handle a plethora of different cheeses and toppings. Try adding Italian-inspired spices like basil, oregano, or rosemary to the dough before baking to give it added flavor. Set aside. Set aside.

Serves 4

Nonstick cooking spray
1¾ cups plus
    2 tablespoons Savory
    Grain-Free Flour Blend
    (page 15)
½ teaspoon salt
½ teaspoon xanthan
    gum
1 (0.25-ounce) package
    instant yeast
⅝ cup warm milk
    (around 115°F)
2 tablespoons unsalted
    butter, softened
1 large egg, room
    temperature
2 tablespoons honey
½ teaspoon apple cider
    vinegar
Toppings, as desired

1. Preheat the oven to 450°F. Spray a large nonstick baking sheet with cooking spray. Set aside.

2. In the bowl of a stand mixer, combine the flour blend, salt, and xanthan gum.

3. Make a small hole with your finger in the middle of the flour mixture and pour the yeast into that hole. Pour the warm milk over the yeast.

4. Add the butter, egg, honey, and vinegar. Using the dough hook attachment, mix until fully combined, about 2 minutes.

5. Spray your hands with cooking spray and place half of the dough on one side of the baking sheet. Flatten it into a large circle, about 10 inches in diameter and ¼ inch thick. Mold and flatten the second half of the dough in the same way on the other side of the baking sheet.

6. Bake on the middle rack for 6 to 7 minutes. Remove from the oven, add your desired toppings, and continue baking baking until your toppings are melty and warm.

Pro Tip: Once you've baked the pizza crust and allowed it to cool to room temperature, you can wrap it tightly with plastic wrap and store it in your refrigerator for up to 24 hours.

Zucchini Bread

Freezable, Refined Sugar—Free
Prep Time: 10 minutes / Bake Time: 1 hour

This is my favorite zucchini bread recipe of all time. It is thick and moist, and the combination of flavors makes it perfect for the dinner table or in a picnic basket for sandwiches. Top it with different types of cheese and your favorite herbs to completely switch up the flavor profile.

Serves 12

Nonstick cooking spray
2¾ cups zucchini, finely chopped in food processor
1½ large eggs, beaten
¼ cup olive oil
¼ cup heavy (whipping) cream
½ large sweet onion, finely chopped in food processor
¾ cup shredded Parmesan cheese
2 cups Grain-Free Biscuit Mix (page 16)

1. Preheat the oven to 350°F. Spray a 9-by-5-inch glass loaf pan with cooking spray. Set aside.

2. Squeeze out any extra moisture in your zucchini by placing it in a kitchen towel and squeezing the bundle over the sink until no liquid drains out.

3. In a large mixing bowl, beat the eggs, oil, and heavy cream until well combined.

4. Add the zucchini, onion, cheese, and biscuit mix and stir until fully combined.

5. Pour the batter into the prepared loaf pan and bake for 50 to 60 minutes or until a toothpick inserted into the center of the loaf comes out clean and the edges of the loaf are golden brown.

6. Allow the bread to cool on a cooling rack before slicing and serving.

Pro Tip: To make this loaf extra-special, when 5 minutes are left in the baking time, add shredded cheese and Italian-inspired seasoning like rosemary, thyme, or basil on top, then continue baking.

Focaccia Bread

Egg-Free, Refined Sugar—Free
Prep Time: 15 minutes / Rise Time: 30 minutes / Bake Time: 26 minutes

A warm, fluffy slice of focaccia bread is always a favorite. I love serving it with a little dipping oil. Simply mix olive oil, balsamic vinegar, and your favorite spices like black pepper, rosemary, garlic, thyme, and fennel.

Serves 12

FOR THE DOUGH

2¼ cups Savory Grain-Free Flour Blend (page 15)

¾ teaspoon salt

2 teaspoons baking powder

1½ cups warm water (around 115°F)

1 (0.25-ounce) package instant yeast

1½ tablespoons honey

5 tablespoons olive oil, divided

Nonstick cooking spray

FOR THE TOPPING

3 tablespoons fresh rosemary

3 tablespoons grated Parmesan cheese

½ teaspoon coarse sea salt

¼ teaspoon freshly ground black pepper

1. In a large mixing bowl, whisk together the flour blend, salt, and baking powder. Set aside.

2. In a small bowl, combine the warm water, yeast, honey, and 2 tablespoons of olive oil. Stir to combine, then set aside to rest for 3 to 5 minutes in a warm spot or until the mixture becomes foamy.

3. Pour the yeast mixture over the flour mixture and stir to combine. Note that the dough will be slightly runny.

4. Cover the bowl with plastic wrap and set it to rise in a warm place for at least 30 minutes. Preheat the oven to 400°F.

5. Generously spray the bottom and sides of a 9-inch pie plate with cooking spray, then drizzle the remaining 3 tablespoons of olive oil evenly on the bottom of the dish.

6. Pour the foamy dough into the prepared pie plate. Sprinkle the surface of the dough with the rosemary, cheese, salt, and pepper.

7. Bake for 22 to 26 minutes or until golden brown. Remove the bread from the oven and let cool at least 10 to 15 minutes before slicing into wedges and eating.

CHAPTER FOUR

COOKIES AND BARS

Cookies, brownies, and perfectly square bars make the best snacks when you're looking for a personal-size sweet treat. The baked goods in this chapter are packed with flavor in every portion. These recipes are simple to make and easy to share—that is, if you don't eat them all first!

Sugar Cookies

Freezable, Refined Sugar–Free
Prep Time: 10 minutes / Chill Time: 1½ to 3 hours / Bake Time: 13 minutes

While your typical sugar cookie can be pretty basic, this grain-free version is anything but. These sugar cookies are delightfully sweet but also easy to pull together. They can even be frozen and thawed when a craving strikes. They are truly the perfect little cookie.

Makes 24 cookies

1 cup monk fruit powdered sugar
1 cup (2 sticks) unsalted butter, softened
1 large egg, beaten
1 tablespoon milk
1 teaspoon pure vanilla extract
1½ cups Sweet Grain-Free Flour Blend (page 14)
½ cup potato starch
½ cup tapioca flour
1 teaspoon baking powder
4 teaspoons xanthan gum
¼ teaspoon salt

1. In a stand mixer, beat the powdered sugar and butter together until smooth. Add the egg, milk, and vanilla and mix until smooth.

2. In a large mixing bowl, combine the flour blend, potato starch, tapioca flour, baking powder, xanthan gum, and salt. Stir until well combined.

3. Slowly add the dry ingredients to the wet ingredients, keeping the mixer on low throughout until the dough has formed. If the dough is sticking to the sides of the bowl, add more of the flour blend, one tablespoon at a time, until the dough no longer sticks to the side of your mixing bowl.

4. Form the dough into a big ball, then wrap it in plastic wrap. Place the dough in the refrigerator to chill for 1½ to 3 hours.

5. Preheat the oven to 375°F and line a baking sheet with parchment paper. Take your chilled dough out of the refrigerator and roll it into golf-ball-size dough balls using your hands. Place the dough balls on the parchment-lined baking sheet, 2 inches apart from one another. Using the palm of your hand, press down on each dough ball until they are about 1/2 inch thick.

6. Place the cookies on the middle oven rack and bake for 11 to 13 minutes or until the edges of the cookies start to turn golden brown. Remove the cookies from the oven and let them cool on the baking sheet for 5 minutes before transferring them to a cooling rack to cool completely.

Comforting Chocolate Chip Cookies

Freezable
Prep Time: 10 minutes / **Chill Time:** 1 hour / **Bake Time:** 15 minutes

My idea of a good chocolate chip cookie is one with slightly crunchy golden edges and a soft center that won't break in half. They should be warm, with melty, gooey chocolate swirls inside. This, my friends, is that cookie.

Makes 12 cookies

8 tablespoons (1 stick) unsalted butter, melted
½ cup light brown coconut sugar
⅓ cup monk fruit baking sugar
1 large egg
1½ teaspoons pure vanilla extract
1⅓ cups Sweet Grain-Free Flour Blend (page 14)
¼ cup potato starch
½ teaspoon baking soda
½ teaspoon salt
⅔ cup semisweet chocolate chips

1. In a stand mixer, beat the butter, coconut sugar, monk fruit sugar, egg, and vanilla at medium speed until smooth.

2. In a small bowl, mix the flour blend, potato starch, baking soda, and salt together. Pour one-third of the flour mixture into the mixer with the wet ingredients and mix on medium speed until smooth. Repeat two more times until all the dry ingredients have been incorporated and a smooth dough forms.

3. Cover the bowl of dough with plastic wrap and chill in the refrigerator for 1 hour. Preheat the oven to 350°F during the last 10 minutes of chilling. Line a baking sheet with parchment paper.

4. Divide the chilled dough into 12 equal parts, then roll each part into a ball. Place the balls on the lined baking sheet. Bake for 13 to 15 minutes or until the cookies have golden edges and risen centers. Allow the cookies to cool on the baking sheet for 5 to 7 minutes, then transfer them to a cooling rack to cool further before enjoying.

Pro Tip: I highly recommend using Lakanto Sugar-Free Chocolate Chips. They're sweetened with monk fruit, keto-friendly, vegan, and delicious.

Peanut Butter Cookies

Dairy-Free, Freezable, Refined Sugar–Free
Prep Time: 5 minutes / Bake Time: 11 minutes

These are my favorite peanut butter cookies. They need only a handful of ingredients and are sweetened just enough to allow for the natural flavors of the peanut butter to shine through. If you want a melt-in-your-mouth cookie that is not overly sugary and is perfectly peanut buttery, then this recipe is for you.

Makes **18 cookies**

1 cup all-natural smooth
   peanut butter
1 cup light brown
   coconut sugar
1 large egg, beaten
1 teaspoon baking soda

1. Preheat the oven to 350°F and line a baking sheet with parchment paper. Set aside.

2. Mix all the ingredients together in a large mixing bowl. Roll the dough into 1-inch balls and place them 3 inches apart from one another on the lined baking sheet.

3. Bake for 9 to 11 minutes or until the edges of each cookie start to turn golden brown. Let the cookies cool on the baking sheet for 5 minutes before transferring them to a cooling rack to cool completely.

Pro Tip: Be careful not to overbake these cookies as they will harden a bit while cooling. Once the outer edges start to turn golden brown, remove them immediately so they can set correctly.

Country Road Bars

Freezable
Prep Time: 15 minutes / Chill Time: 3 hours

When I'm craving something sweet and salty, I turn to this country road bar. It has layers of sweet chocolate on top of a smooth cookie-like crust, swirled with crunchy cashew pieces, all topped with large flakes of sea salt. I love to freeze mine and eat them chilled.

Makes **12 to 16 bars**

FOR THE PEANUT BUTTER CRUST

2 cups peanut butter
1½ cups light brown coconut sugar
1½ cups monk fruit powdered sugar
6 tablespoons (¾ stick) unsalted butter, melted

FOR THE MISSISSIPPI MUD TOPPING

9 ounces semisweet dark chocolate baking chips
¾ cup salted, roasted cashews, coarsely chopped
Coarse sea salt

1. Line an 8-inch square aluminum foil pan with parchment paper and set aside.

2. To make the peanut butter crust, in a medium mixing bowl, stir the peanut butter, coconut sugar, powdered sugar, and butter together until well blended. Press the mixture evenly into the bottom of the parchment-lined pan.

3. To make the Mississippi mud topping, heat the chocolate chips in a medium mixing bowl in the microwave according to package instructions until melted. Pour half of the melted chocolate over the peanut butter crust and spread it out evenly.

4. Sprinkle the cashew pieces over the melted chocolate layer, then drizzle the remaining melted chocolate on top. Sprinkle with a pinch or two of sea salt.

5. Refrigerate until firm, 2 to 3 hours, or freeze for 30 to 60 minutes.

6. Cut into squares and enjoy!

Ingredient Tip: I highly recommend using Guittard Santé Dark Chocolate Baking Chips here. They are the best-tasting keto and paleo-friendly dark chocolate baking chips I have found.

Lemon Bars

Prep Time: 15 minutes / Chill Time: 2 hours / Bake Time: 1 hour 10 minutes

Summers are best with a lemon bar in your hand. These citrus bars have a soft cookie crust and are topped with a lemon layer that is baked to perfection. Allow the lemon bars to chill before cutting them; serve well chilled for the ultimate refreshment.

Makes 24 bars

1 cup almond flour

½ cup plus 1 tablespoon tapioca flour, divided

½ cup powdered sugar, plus more for topping

4 tablespoons (½ stick) unsalted butter, softened

1 teaspoon pure vanilla extract

2 tablespoons plain Greek yogurt

4 large eggs

1 (14-ounce) can sweetened condensed milk

⅓ cup freshly squeezed lemon juice

⅓ cup freshly squeezed lime juice

1 teaspoon baking powder

⅛ teaspoon salt

3 drops yellow food coloring (optional)

1. Preheat the oven to 350°F.

2. In a medium mixing bowl, combine the almond flour, ½ cup of tapioca flour, the powdered sugar, butter, vanilla, and yogurt. Mix until the ingredients turn into a crumbly mixture.

3. Press the mixture into the bottom of an ungreased 8- or 9-inch square baking pan and bake for 20 minutes. Set aside and let cool to room temperature.

4. While the crust is cooling, in a medium mixing bowl, beat the eggs and sweetened condensed milk together until they are slightly fluffy, 1 to 2 minutes on medium-high speed with a hand or stand mixer. Add the lemon juice, lime juice, the remaining 1 tablespoon of tapioca flour, the baking powder, salt, and yellow food coloring, if using.

5. Pour this mixture over the cooled crust and bake for another 20 minutes. Then, cover the bars with aluminum foil and bake for another 30 minutes or until the filling is set. The outer crust should be slightly golden brown and the center firm to the touch.

6. Chill the lemon bars in the refrigerator for 1 to 2 hours. Cut the bars into squares and sprinkle with additional powdered sugar.

White Chocolate Chip Brownies

Freezable
Prep Time: 10 minutes / **Bake Time:** 37 minutes

Decadent brownies are always the best kind. These are soft, moist, and sprinkled with white chocolate chips throughout. Serve them warm with fresh berries, topped with homemade whipped cream or ice cream, or just scarf them down plain. No matter which way you serve them, they'll be devoured in seconds.

Makes **16 bars**

12 tablespoons
  (1½ sticks) unsalted
  butter, melted
1 cup monk fruit baking
  sugar
½ cup light brown
  coconut sugar
1½ teaspoons pure
  vanilla extract
3 large eggs
½ cup cocoa powder
¼ cup tapioca flour
¼ cup coconut flour
1 tablespoon
  xanthan gum
½ cup white chocolate
  chips
¼ teaspoon sea salt

1. Preheat the oven to 350°F, then line an 8-by-8-inch baking pan with parchment paper. Set aside.

2. In a large mixing bowl, combine the butter, monk fruit sugar, coconut sugar, and vanilla. Add the eggs and stir until well combined and smooth. Add the cocoa powder and stir again. Add the tapioca flour, coconut flour, and xanthan gum and stir until a smooth batter forms. Fold in the chocolate chips.

3. Pour the brownie batter evenly into the lined baking pan. Sprinkle the batter with the sea salt and bake on the middle rack of the oven for 34 to 37 minutes. The brownies will be done when the outer edges are dark and firm to the touch. A toothpick inserted into the center should come out clean.

4. Allow the brownies to cool in the pan to room temperature. Cut into 16 squares and enjoy.

Recipe Tip: Try swapping out the white chocolate chips for dark chocolate chips, butterscotch chips, or even minty chips.

Quinoa Crunch Bars

Freezable
Prep Time: 10 minutes / **Rest Time:** 5 minutes / **Bake Time:** 37 minutes

These easy-to-make bars are ridiculously tasty in the mornings, especially while still warm from baking or warmed up in the microwave for a few seconds. They are also easily customizable. I like to add my latest craving to them, whether that's white chocolate chips, caramel pieces, marshmallows, or nuts.

Makes 12 bars

1½ cups cooked gluten-free quinoa
⅔ cup all-natural peanut butter
½ cup fresh honey
2 large eggs
⅔ cup natural applesauce
1½ teaspoons pure vanilla extract
¾ cup Grain-Free Biscuit Mix (page 16)
½ cup coconut flour
1 teaspoon baking soda
1½ teaspoons ground cinnamon
½ cup add-ins, such as chocolate chips, dried fruit, or nuts

1. Preheat the oven to 375°F. Line a 9-by-13-inch baking pan with parchment paper. Set aside.

2. In a large mixing bowl, combine the quinoa, peanut butter, honey, eggs, applesauce, and vanilla. Add the biscuit mix, flour, baking soda, and cinnamon. Mix well. Let the batter rest for 5 minutes.

3. Pour the mixture into the lined pan and gently press it flat.

4. Bake for 32 to 37 minutes or until the edges start to become golden brown.

5. Allow the bars to cool in the pan for 5 minutes before cutting into squares and serving.

Ingredient Tip: If you'd like to make your add-ins a bit healthier, try dried fruit like raisins, cranberries, or even banana pieces.

Chocolate-Dipped Mint Cookies

Freezable
Prep Time: 15 minutes / **Chill Time:** 60 minutes / **Bake Time:** 20 minutes

One of my favorite flavor combinations is chocolate and mint. It's the perfect mix of refreshing and sweet, simple yet surprising. In this recipe, layers of smooth chocolate flirt with the crunch of chocolate-mint cookies. Their flavor and texture are satisfying, bite after bite.

Makes 60 cookies

1 cup Sweet Grain-Free Flour Blend (page 14)
½ cup unsweetened cocoa powder
½ teaspoon baking powder
½ teaspoon baking soda
¼ teaspoon salt
5 tablespoons unsalted butter, softened
¾ cup granulated sugar
1 large egg, room temperature
1 large egg yolk, room temperature
1 teaspoon pure vanilla extract
2 teaspoons peppermint extract, divided
16 to 18 ounces chocolate chips

1. In a large mixing bowl, combine the flour blend, cocoa powder, baking powder, baking soda, and salt.

2. In a stand mixer, beat the butter and granulated sugar until well combined and smooth, 1 to 3 minutes on medium speed. Add the whole egg and mix well. Add the egg yolk and mix well again. Beat in the vanilla and 1½ teaspoons of peppermint extract until completely combined, 1 to 2 minutes.

3. Slowly beat the dry ingredient mixture into the wet ingredients. Once fully combined, the dough will be thick and sticky.

4. Roll the dough into a large ball, then place that ball between two pieces of wax paper. Flatten it out between the wax paper sheets and place it in the refrigerator to chill for 20 to 30 minutes or up to overnight.

5. Line two baking sheets with parchment paper. Roll the dough out until it's ⅛ inch thick. Using a flour-dipped cookie cutter or the top of a small cup, punch out 1½-inch circular cookies. Place them on the lined baking sheets. Chill for another 15 to 30 minutes. Preheat the oven to 350°F. Let the rest of the dough continue chilling, then repeat.

6. Bake for 10 to 12 minutes, turning the baking sheets front to back halfway through. Remove the cookies from the oven and allow them to cool completely.

7. Melt the chocolate chips in the microwave according to the package instructions. Once melted, stir in the remaining ½ teaspoon of peppermint extract. Dip each cookie into the mint chocolate, using a fork to flip the cookies so they're fully coated. Let the excess chocolate drip from each cookie, then scrape the bottoms with a fork before putting them on a fresh piece of parchment paper to harden. Serve once the chocolate has set.

Preparation Tip: If your cookies don't completely harden while at room temperature, place them in the refrigerator for a quick, refreshing fix.

CHAPTER FIVE

CAKES AND CUPCAKES

Cakes and cupcakes should be fluffy and moist. However, many grain-free cakes and cupcakes often turn out crumbly and dry. It doesn't have to be this way. The cakes and cupcakes in this chapter are both spongy and soft without any grittiness. Enjoy every bite.

Coffee Cake Cupcakes

Refined Sugar–Free
Prep Time: 15 minutes / Bake Time: 50 minutes

Coffee cake cupcakes may be hard to say, but they're not hard to bake. Coffee cake is typically eaten at breakfast and pairs well with your favorite cup of joe. These tender, sweet cupcakes are topped with a cinnamon-sugar crumble baked into a slightly crisped, golden-brown crust—a perfect bite to start your day.

Makes **12 cupcakes**

FOR THE COFFEE CAKE
1½ cups monk fruit powdered sugar
1½ cup Grain-Free Biscuit Mix (page 16)
½ cup potato starch
¼ cup tapioca flour
1 tablespoon baking powder
2 teaspoons xanthan gum
¾ teaspoon salt
3 large eggs
¾ cup whole milk
12 tablespoons (1½ sticks) unsalted butter, softened
2 tablespoons almond extract

TO MAKE THE COFFEE CAKE

1. Preheat the oven to 350°F, then line a 12-cup muffin tin with cupcake liners. Set aside.

2. In a large mixing bowl, combine the powdered sugar, biscuit mix, potato starch, tapioca flour, baking powder, xanthan gum, and salt. Mix well. Add the eggs, milk, butter, and almond extract, then stir until a smooth batter forms.

3. Fill the cupcake liners two-thirds full of batter. Bake the cupcakes on the middle rack for 10 minutes.

TO MAKE THE CINNAMON CRUMBLE

4. While the batter is cooking, create the cinnamon crumble by combining the brown sugar, powdered sugar, cinnamon, and butter in a medium mixing bowl. Once combined, add the flour blend and stir until just combined.

FOR THE CINNAMON CRUMBLE

1 cup packed light brown sugar

½ cup monk fruit powdered sugar

1 tablespoon ground cinnamon

8 tablespoons (1 stick) unsalted butter, softened

½ cup Sweet Grain-Free Flour Blend (page 14)

5. Remove the muffin tin from the oven, then sprinkle an even, thin layer of the crumble on top of the cupcakes. Cover them with aluminum foil, then bake for another 35 to 40 minutes or until the edges and top of the cupcakes are a rich medium brown and a toothpick inserted into the center of the cupcakes is pulled out clean.

6. Remove the cupcakes from the oven and allow them to cool for 10 minutes before serving.

Troubleshooting Tip: There will likely be spillover of the crumble topping as it heats and melts. I highly recommend placing a baking sheet underneath the muffin tin as it bakes to collect any sugary drippings.

Banana Split Cupcakes

Dairy-Free Option
Prep Time: 15 minutes / Bake Time: 23 minutes

Don't throw away overly ripe bananas. Use them for the moistest, softest banana-flavored cupcakes instead. These cupcakes are tender with hints of banana in every bite. Top them off with smooth chocolate frosting and fresh strawberry slices for all the flavor of a classic banana split.

Makes 12 cupcakes

1²⁄₃ cups Sweet Grain-Free Flour Blend (page 14)

1 cup monk fruit baking sugar

1 teaspoon baking soda

¼ teaspoon baking powder

½ teaspoon salt

2 large eggs

⅓ cup water

⅓ cup unsalted butter, melted

2½ very ripe medium bananas, mashed

1 cup store-bought chocolate frosting

1 cup fresh sliced strawberries

1. Preheat the oven to 350°F, then line a 12-cup muffin tin with cupcake liners. Set aside.

2. In a large mixing bowl, combine the flour blend, sugar, baking soda, baking powder, salt, eggs, water, butter, and bananas. Allow to sit for 5 minutes.

3. Fill each cupcake liner halfway full of batter. Bake for 20 to 23 minutes or until the edges are golden brown.

4. Remove the cupcakes from the oven and allow to cool for 5 to 10 minutes in the muffin tin before moving them to a cooling rack to cool completely.

5. Spread the chocolate frosting on each cooled cupcake and place a strawberry slice on top.

Substitution Tip: Make this recipe dairy-free by replacing the butter with dairy-free butter.

Dark Chocolate Cupcakes

Freezable, Refined Sugar–Free
Prep Time: 15 minutes / **Bake Time:** 20 minutes

Hoping to impress your friends and family with your baking skills? Look no further. These cupcakes are easy enough for a beginner but taste like the work of a professional baker. They're also the perfect homemade gift idea for any chocolate lover in your life.

Makes **12 cupcakes**

FOR THE CAKE
1¾ cups Grain-Free
   Biscuit Mix (page 16)
¾ cup cocoa powder
½ teaspoon salt
¼ teaspoon baking
   powder
¼ teaspoon baking soda
2 large eggs
1 cup whole milk
½ cup canola oil
1½ tablespoons pure
   vanilla extract

FOR THE FROSTING
1½ cups (3 sticks)
   unsalted butter,
   softened
5 to 7 tablespoons milk
3 cups monk fruit
   powdered sugar
1 cup cocoa powder
¼ cup melted dark
   chocolate

TO MAKE THE CAKE

1. Preheat the oven to 350°F, then line a 12-cup muffin tin with cupcake liners. Set aside.

2. In a large mixing bowl, combine the biscuit mix, cocoa powder, salt, baking powder, and baking soda. Mix well. Add the eggs, milk, oil, and vanilla, then stir until well combined.

3. Pour the batter evenly into the cupcake liners. Bake for about 20 minutes or until a toothpick inserted into the center comes out clean.

4. Place the cupcake tin on a cooling rack and allow to cool for 10 minutes. Then, remove the cupcakes from the muffin tin and let cool to room temperature.

TO MAKE THE FROSTING

5. Beat the butter in a stand mixer until smooth. Add the milk and beat again. Slowly add the powdered sugar and cocoa powder and beat until combined. Add the melted chocolate and beat for another 2 minutes or until a thick frosting consistency is reached.

6. Frost the cupcakes once they have fully cooled to room temperature.

Carrot Cake

Dairy-Free Option, Freezable, Refined Sugar–Free
Prep Time: 10 minutes / **Bake Time:** 22 minutes

If you're looking for a cake that isn't too sweet, this mellow carrot cake is for you. It's simple to make and yields an incredibly moist and light cake with a tender golden crust on top. I like to top my cake with homemade whipped cream and a light drizzle of honey or pure maple syrup.

Serves 12

Nonstick cooking spray
1 cup almond flour
1 cup coconut flour
2 tablespoons xanthan gum
1 tablespoon baking powder
1½ teaspoons baking soda
1¼ teaspoons ground cinnamon
¾ cup canola oil
3 tablespoons unsalted butter, softened
2 large eggs, beaten
1 cup monk fruit baking sugar
½ cup water
2 teaspoons pure vanilla extract
2 cups finely grated carrots
1 cup finely grated coconut

1. Preheat the oven to 350°F. Spray a 9-by-9-inch non-stick baking pan with cooking spray and set aside.

2. In a small mixing bowl, combine the almond flour, coconut flour, xanthan gum, baking powder, baking soda, and cinnamon.

3. In a large mixing bowl, combine the oil, butter, eggs, sugar, water, and vanilla. Add the carrots and coconut. Stir well.

4. Slowly add the dry ingredients to the wet ingredients and combine with a hand or stand mixer for about 1 minute or until a batter forms.

5. Pour the batter into the prepared baking pan and bake for 20 to 22 minutes or until the top is golden brown and a toothpick inserted into the center comes out clean.

6. Let the cake cool completely before applying any toppings.

Substitution Tip: To make this recipe dairy-free, use dairy-free butter.

Quick Strawberry Shortcake

Refined Sugar–Free
Prep Time: 10 minutes / **Bake Time:** 13 minutes

Strawberry shortcake has been one of my favorite desserts ever since I was a little girl. This 25-minute recipe serves up soft, fluffy, decadent strawberry cakes topped with fresh-cut strawberries and creamy whipped cream for a flavor-packed dessert made in minutes.

Serves 2

2 tablespoons coconut flour
2 tablespoons almond flour
1 tablespoon coconut sugar
½ teaspoon baking powder
Pinch salt
¼ cup plain almond milk
1 large egg, beaten
¼ teaspoon strawberry extract
Whipped cream, for topping
1 cup sliced strawberries

1. Preheat the oven to 350°F.

2. In a medium mixing bowl, combine the coconut flour, almond flour, sugar, baking powder, and salt.

3. Add the almond milk, egg, and strawberry extract. Mix well, then let sit for 5 minutes for the flours to expand.

4. Pour the dough into two 4-ounce ramekins and bake for 11 to 13 minutes, until the outside starts to turn a light golden brown.

5. Let the cakes cool for 5 minutes. Serve warm with whipped cream and strawberries on top.

Baking Tip: If you don't have ramekins, you can use oven-safe coffee cups or bowls instead. Mugs are especially easy to move in and out of the oven, due to their handles.

Simple Cheesecake

Dairy-Free Option
Prep Time: 20 minutes / **Chill Time:** 4 to 6 hours

One of the comfort foods that I missed most when first becoming grain-free and gluten-free was a classic vanilla cheesecake. Fortunately, this cheesecake is thick and rich with its fluffy yet dense core and sweet, soft crust. As a bonus, it's easily customizable, so it's bound to become one of your favorites.

Serves 10

FOR THE CRUST
2½ cups Crispy Sweet Cinnamon Flatbread (page 26) crumbs, crushed
⅓ cup light brown coconut sugar
10 tablespoons unsalted butter, melted

FOR THE FILLING
3 (8-ounce) packages cream cheese, softened
½ cup granulated sugar
5 tablespoons powdered sugar
¼ cup sour cream
1½ teaspoons pure vanilla extract
1¼ cups heavy (whipping) cream

TO MAKE THE CRUST

1. Mix the flatbread crumbs, coconut sugar, and butter together in a medium mixing bowl. Pour the mixture into the bottom of a springform pan and press it down firmly. Place the crust in the freezer while making the cheesecake filling, 10 to 15 minutes.

TO MAKE THE FILLING

2. Whip the cream cheese, granulated sugar, powdered sugar, sour cream, and vanilla together in a stand mixer until well blended and smooth, 3 to 4 minutes.

3. Pour in the heavy cream and whip the mixture on medium speed until stiff peaks form, 3 to 5 minutes. Pour the cream cheese filling into the pan with the crust.

4. Cover the pan and place in the refrigerator to chill for 4 to 6 hours before serving.

Variation Tip: Try your hand at other flavors of cheesecake by substituting strawberry extract or lemon extract for the vanilla extract.

Substitution Tip: To make a dairy-free version, substitute dairy-free butter for the butter, dairy-free cream cheese for the cream cheese, dairy-free sour cream for the sour cream, and dairy-free cream for the heavy cream.

Simple Pound Cake

Prep Time: 10 minutes / Bake Time: 65 minutes

Every birthday growing up, I asked for a pound cake with strawberries and whipped cream. It is my favorite cake in the entire world. So when I went gluten-free and grain-free, I was sad to lose it. After years of trial and error, I have finally made a sweet and moist pound cake with all the weight of a regular pound cake but none of the grain or gluten.

Serves 12

Nonstick cooking spray
8 tablespoons (1 stick) unsalted butter, softened
1¼ cups granulated sugar
½ teaspoon salt
3 large eggs
1 tablespoon almond extract
1¼ cups Grain-Free Biscuit Mix (page 16)
½ teaspoon baking powder
⅓ cup heavy (whipping) cream

Substitution Tip: If you don't have almond extract in your pantry, use 1 tablespoon pure vanilla extract.

1. Preheat the oven to 325°F, then spray a 9-by-5-inch nonstick metal loaf pan generously with cooking spray. Set aside.

2. In a stand mixer, beat the butter until smooth. Add the sugar and salt and mix for 1 minute. Add the eggs and almond extract and mix until just combined.

3. In a small bowl, mix the biscuit mix and baking powder together. Slowly add one-third of the biscuit mixture to the mixer bowl on low speed until it has all been added. Repeat two more times until all ingredients are just combined.

4. Add the heavy cream and stir until just combined.

5. Pour the mixture into the prepared baking pan, place on the center rack of the oven, and bake for 40 minutes. Then, cover the pan with aluminum foil and bake for another 20 to 25 minutes or until a toothpick inserted into the center of the cake comes out clean.

6. Remove the pound cake from the oven and allow it to cool to room temperature. Slice and serve.

Lemon Drop Cake

Freezable, Refined Sugar–Free

Prep Time: 15 minutes / Bake Time: 45 minutes / Set Time: 30 to 60 minutes

There is something so refreshing about citrus-flavored baked goods. This light, fluffy, and moist cake is covered in a sweet lemon glaze for a blast of citrus flavor. I like to serve this cake with seasonal berries.

Serves **8**

FOR THE LEMON CAKE
Nonstick cooking spray
1 cup Sweet Grain-Free Flour Blend (page 14)
½ cup Grain-Free Biscuit Mix (page 16)
1 cup monk fruit sugar
2 teaspoons baking powder
½ teaspoon salt
2 large eggs
½ cup whole milk
8 tablespoons (1 stick) unsalted butter, softened
3 tablespoons freshly squeezed lemon juice

FOR THE LEMON ICING
¾ cup monk fruit powdered sugar
4 to 5 tablespoons freshly squeezed lemon juice

TO MAKE THE LEMON CAKE

1. Preheat the oven to 350°F, then spray a 9" x 5" 1-pound loaf pan with cooking spray. Set aside.

2. In a large mixing bowl, combine the flour blend, biscuit mix, sugar, baking powder, and salt, then mix well. Add the eggs, milk, butter, and lemon juice, then stir until well combined and a smooth batter forms.

3. Pour the batter into the prepared pan and bake on the middle rack for 20 minutes. Then, cover the pan with aluminum foil and bake for another 25 minute, until the edges and top of the loaf are golden brown and a toothpick inserted into the center of the loaf comes out clean.

4. Remove the pan from the oven and allow to cool for 10 minutes. Remove the loaf from the pan and let cool to room temperature on a cooling rack.

TO MAKE THE LEMON ICING

5. While the loaf is cooling, mix the powdered sugar and lemon juice in a small bowl. Pour the icing over the room-temperature loaf and allow to harden for 30 to 60 minutes. Slice into pieces 1 to 1½ inch thick and serve.

Vanilla Mug Cake

Dairy-Free Option, Refined Sugar–Free
Prep Time: 5 minutes / Cook Time: 5 minutes

This easy and cute dessert doesn't need much of an introduction. Soft, fluffy, vanilla-flavored cake comes out steamy hot from the microwave and can be topped with fresh berries, whipped cream, and sprinkles for a flavor-packed, single-serving dessert baked in minutes.

Serves 1

3 tablespoons coconut flour
1½ tablespoons almond flour
1 tablespoon coconut sugar
½ teaspoon baking powder
Pinch salt
¼ cup plain almond milk
1 large egg, beaten
1½ teaspoons pure vanilla extract
Berries, for topping (optional)
Whipped cream, for topping (optional)

1. In a medium mixing bowl, combine the coconut flour, almond flour, coconut sugar, baking powder, and salt.

2. Add the almond milk, egg, and vanilla and mix well. Let sit for 5 minutes for the flours to expand.

3. Pour the batter into a microwave-safe coffee mug and microwave on full power for 3 to 5 minutes. Watch the cake carefully in order not to overcook. When done, a toothpick inserted into the center should come out clean.

4. Let the cake cool for 5 minutes. Serve warm with berries and whipped cream on top, if you like.

CHAPTER SIX

PASTRIES AND MUFFINS

There's no better way to wake up in the morning than with the aroma of a freshly baked pastry or muffin coming out of the oven. Add a sliver of butter or a drizzle of honey to these treats while they're still warm so it melts into every bite. Pair these breakfast goodies with your favorite cup of coffee or tea.

Cinnamon-Sugar-Rolled Custard Coins

Refined Sugar–Free
Prep Time: 10 minutes / **Cook Time:** 40 minutes

This recipe turned into my favorite and most delicious kitchen fail of all time. While trying to make a sweet version of a popover that went terribly wrong (that is, flat as flat could be), I came across the making of the first-ever custard coins. These dense, doughy coin-shaped pastries are baked to golden perfection and then rolled in cinnamon-sugar. They're delicious served warm but are also good at room temperature or even chilled.

Makes 12 coins

Nonstick cooking spray
½ cup heavy (whipping) cream
8 tablespoons (1 stick) unsalted butter, cubed
1½ tablespoons monk fruit baking sugar
1 teaspoon xanthan gum
Pinch salt
½ cup Sweet Grain-Free Flour Blend (page 14)
2 large eggs, room temperature
1 large egg white, room temperature
½ cup light brown coconut sugar
1 teaspoon ground cinnamon

1. Preheat the oven to 400°F, then grease a 12-cup muffin tin with cooking spray. Set aside.

2. In a small saucepan, combine the heavy cream, butter, sugar, xanthan gum, and salt. Stir over medium-low heat until the sugar dissolves completely, 4 to 5 minutes. Bring the mixture to medium-high heat until it begins to boil rapidly.

3. Remove the pan from the heat, then pour in the flour blend. Place the pan back on the stovetop over medium heat and stir continuously until the mixture thickens, 1 to 2 minutes. Remove the pan from the heat and allow to cool for 3 to 4 minutes.

4. Add the eggs and egg white and stir by hand until the mixture is smooth, thick, and shiny.

5. Fill each cup of the greased muffin tin two-thirds full with the dough. Use one finger dipped in water to smooth any points on each top.

6. Place the custard coins in the oven and bake for 5 minutes. Turn the heat down to 325°F and continue baking for 10 to 12 minutes or until golden brown on top.

7. Mix the coconut sugar and cinnamon in a small bowl. Remove the custard coins and carefully roll them in the cinnamon-sugar mixture. Allow them to cool to room temperature before serving. Store in an airtight food-safe container or bag in the refrigerator for up to 4 days.

Banana Bread Doughnuts

Freezable, Refined Sugar–Free
Prep Time: 10 minutes / Bake Time: 17 minutes

There is no better way to eat banana bread than in doughnut form. These delicious rings of warm bread melt bananas into a sweet batter and are baked into fluffy heaven. Taking them out of the oven is a joy as the sweet, comforting aromas fill your kitchen. Drizzle them with honey or pure maple syrup or add a dollop of whipped cream to take these doughnuts over the top.

Makes 6 doughnuts

Nonstick cooking spray
1⅔ cups Grain-Free Biscuit Mix (page 16)
1 cup monk fruit baking sugar
1 teaspoon baking soda
¼ teaspoon baking powder
½ teaspoon salt
2 large eggs
⅓ cup water
⅓ cup unsalted butter, melted
2½ very ripe medium bananas, mashed

1. Preheat the oven to 350°F. Spray a 6-ring nonstick doughnut pan with cooking spray and set aside.

2. In a large mixing bowl, combine the biscuit mix, sugar, baking soda, baking powder, salt, eggs, water, butter, and bananas. Mix together and allow to sit for 5 minutes.

3. Add the batter to the doughnut pan, filling each ring halfway. Bake for 15 to 17 minutes or until the edges of the doughnuts turn a nice golden brown.

4. Remove the plan from the oven and allow the doughnuts to cool for 5 to 10 minutes before moving them to a cooling rack.

Variation Tip: This recipe is fantastic when made into mini bread loaves for brunch or as gifts for parties or holidays. Fill the mini loaf liners two-thirds full and bake at 350°F for 21 to 23 minutes or until the edges are nicely golden brown. Keep the mini loaves in their cups when serving or gift wrapped in cellophane and tied with a ribbon.

Mini Blueberry Muffins

Freezable, Refined Sugar–Free
Prep Time: 15 minutes / Bake Time: 18 minutes

When I was growing up, my dad and I made blueberry muffins together on the weekends. He would prop me up on the kitchen counter and help me pour all the ingredients into a big mixing bowl. I'd spill muffin mix with every swirl of the spatula. These happy memories come back each time I make this recipe.

Makes **18 mini muffins**

Nonstick cooking spray
½ cup coconut flour
1 teaspoon baking soda
½ teaspoon baking powder
2 tablespoons coconut sugar
¼ teaspoon salt
2 large eggs, room temperature and beaten
1 teaspoon pure vanilla extract
1 tablespoon apple cider vinegar
1 tablespoon unsalted butter, softened
½ cup vanilla almond milk, room temperature
⅓ cup honey
⅓ cup coconut oil, melted
⅔ cup fresh blueberries

1. Preheat the oven to 350°F. Line 18 cups of a 24-cup mini muffin tin with cupcake liners or spray with cooking spray. Set aside.

2. In a medium mixing bowl, combine the flour, baking soda, baking powder, sugar, and salt.

3. In a large mixing bowl, combine the eggs, vanilla, vinegar, butter, almond milk, honey, and oil.

4. Slowly add the dry ingredients to the bowl with the wet ingredients. Using a hand or stand mixer, mix until well combined. Allow the dough to set and thicken for 5 minutes.

5. Fold in the blueberries, then fill each mini muffin cup three-quarters full of the batter.

6. Bake for 13 to 18 minutes or until the edges are golden brown and a toothpick inserted into the center of a muffin comes out clean.

7. Allow the muffins to cool slightly before taking them out of the tin and allowing them to cool on a cooling rack.

Lemon, Poppy Seed, and Thyme Scones

Freezable, Refined Sugar–Free
Prep Time: 20 minutes / Chill Time: 10 minutes / Bake Time: 10 minutes

Refreshing lemon flavors are coupled with the slight crunch of poppy seeds in this easy scone recipe. Feel free to turn these scones into cookies by scooping the batter into muffin cups that have been sprayed with cooking spray. I like to fancy my scones up by serving them with a small sprig of fresh rosemary on top.

Makes 10 to 12 scones

2¼ cups Grain-Free
  Biscuit Mix (page 16)
3 tablespoons monk
  fruit baking sugar
1 teaspoon baking
  powder
½ teaspoon salt
4 tablespoons (½ stick)
  unsalted butter
1 large egg, beaten
⅔ cup heavy (whipping)
  cream, plus more for
  brushing
1 teaspoon freshly
  squeezed lemon juice
1 teaspoon black poppy
  seeds
1 teaspoon fresh thyme,
  finely chopped

1. Preheat the oven to 400°F, then line a baking sheet with parchment paper. Set aside.

2. In a large mixing bowl, stir the biscuit mix, sugar, baking powder, and salt until well mixed. Add the butter, egg, heavy cream, lemon juice, poppy seeds, and thyme. Stir until smooth and well combined.

3. Roll the dough out into a 1½-inch-thick rectangle and cut it into circles with a 2-inch round cookie cutter to make 10 to 12 scones.

4. Place the scones on the parchment-lined baking sheet, 1 to 2 inches apart from each other. Place the baking sheet in the refrigerator for 10 minutes to chill the dough. Once chilled, brush the top of each scone with some heavy cream.

5. Bake the dough on the middle rack for about 10 minutes or until the edges of each scone start to turn golden brown.

6. Remove the scones from the oven and allow them to cool to room temperature before serving.

Orange Blossom Muffin Bites

Freezable, Refined Sugar–Free

Prep Time: 5 minutes / **Bake Time:** 11 minutes / **Set Time:** 1 hour

One of my younger brother's favorite muffins growing up was the orange blossom muffins from this specific bakery in Texas. Decades later, a friend happened to mention them at a party, and my fond memories of biting into those moist, orange-flavored muffins with their thick orange glaze came right back. My craving was so intense that I developed this refreshingly sweet recipe.

Makes **24 muffin bites**

FOR THE MUFFINS

Nonstick cooking spray

1 cup **Grain Free Biscuit Mix (page 16)**

½ cup whole milk

2 small eggs, beaten

4 tablespoons (½ stick) unsalted butter, melted

½ teaspoon orange extract

2 tablespoons milk powder

FOR THE GLAZE

1½ cups monk fruit powdered sugar

2 teaspoon orange extract

2½ tablespoons vegetable oil

3 to 4 tablespoons water

TO MAKE THE MUFFINS

1. Preheat the oven to 350°F, then spray a 24-cup mini muffin tin with cooking spray. Set aside.

2. In a large mixing bowl, combine the biscuit mix, milk, eggs, butter, orange extract, and milk powder. Beat well with a hand or stand mixer for 2 minutes.

3. Spoon the batter into the prepared mini muffin cups, filling each muffin cup halfway. Bake for 9 to 11 minutes, until the edges start to turn golden brown. Remove the muffins from the oven and allow them to cool to room temperature.

TO MAKE THE GLAZE

4. While the muffins are cooling, make the glaze by combining the powdered sugar, orange extract, oil, and water in a small bowl. Mix well with a spoon until smooth.

5. Dip each muffin into the orange glaze, covering as much of the muffin as possible.

6. Place each glazed muffin on a cooling rack with a baking sheet underneath to collect any drips. Let the glaze set for about 1 hour.

Powdered Sugar Popovers

Refined Sugar–Free
Prep Time: 20 minutes / **Cook Time:** 24 minutes

To me, popovers have always been a special treat. These extra-fluffy, muffin-like pastries can be served with sweet or savory toppings. No matter how you like them, everyone agrees that the best popovers are soft and billowy on top with a nice golden crust and large air pockets within. This recipe delivers all these things. Plus, the powdered sugar is simple but sophisticated and provides a perfectly sweet finish.

Makes 12 popovers

Nonstick cooking spray
½ cup heavy (whipping) cream
8 tablespoons (1 stick) unsalted butter, cubed
1½ tablespoons monk fruit baking sugar
1 teaspoon xanthan gum
Pinch salt
¾ cup Grain-Free Biscuit Mix (page 16)
2 large eggs, room temperature
1 large egg white, room temperature
8 to 10 tablespoons monk fruit powdered sugar

1. Preheat the oven to 400°F, then grease a 12-cup muffin tin with cooking spray. Set aside.

2. In a small saucepan, combine the heavy cream, butter, baking sugar, xanthan gum, and salt. Stir over medium-low heat until the sugar dissolves completely, 4 to 5 minutes. Turn the heat to medium-high and bring the mixture to a rapid boil.

3. Remove the pan from the heat and add the biscuit mix. Place the pan back on the stovetop and cook over medium heat, stirring continuously until the mixture balls up and the flour is cooked, 1 to 2 minutes. Remove the pan from the heat and allow to cool for 3 to 4 minutes.

4. Add the eggs and egg white, and stir by hand until the mixture is smooth, thick, and shiny.

5. Fill the greased muffin cups two-thirds full with the dough. Use one finger dipped in water to smooth any points on each top.

6. Place the pan in the oven and bake for 5 minutes. Turn the heat down to 325°F and continue baking for 10 to 12 minutes or until golden brown on top.

7. Remove the popovers from the oven and immediately sprinkle them with powdered sugar.

8. Cut a very small slit into one side of each puff to allow steam to vent and let cool to room temperature before serving.

Glazed Chocolate Doughnut Holes

Freezable, Refined Sugar–Free
Prep Time: 15 minutes / **Bake Time:** 10 minutes / **Set Time:** 1 hour

Glazed doughnut holes are the best because you can pop them in your mouth on-the-go. You can make your glaze as thick or thin as you like by adjusting the liquid. I like my glaze thick, hugging my doughnut tight.

Makes
24 doughnut holes

FOR THE DOUGHNUT HOLES

Nonstick cooking spray
1 cup Grain-Free Biscuit Mix (page 16)
½ cup monk fruit baking sugar
¼ cup cocoa powder
½ teaspoon baking powder
½ teaspoon baking soda
⅛ teaspoon salt
1 large egg, room temperature and beaten
6 tablespoons milk of choice, room temperature
2 tablespoons Greek yogurt
1½ tablespoons unsalted butter, melted
1 teaspoon pure vanilla extract

TO MAKE THE DOUGHNUT HOLES

1. Preheat the oven to 350°F, then spray a 24-count mini muffin tin with cooking spray. Set aside.

2. In a medium mixing bowl, combine the biscuit mix, sugar, cocoa powder, baking powder, baking soda, and salt. Stir well and set aside.

3. In a medium mixing bowl, combine the egg, milk, yogurt, butter, and vanilla and stir well. Add the dry ingredients to the bowl with the wet ingredients and stir until just combined. Do not overstir!

4. Pour the batter into the pan, filling each cup halfway full. Bake for 7 to 10 minutes or until the edges of each doughnut hole begin to become slightly darker brown. Remove the doughnuts from the oven and allow them to cool to room temperature.

FOR THE ICING GLAZE

1 cup monk fruit
  powdered sugar
2 tablespoons milk
1 teaspoon pure vanilla
  extract

TO MAKE THE ICING GLAZE

5. While the doughnut holes are cooling, make the glaze by combining the powdered sugar, milk, and vanilla in a mixing bowl. Stir until smooth.

6. Once the holes are cooled, dunk each hole into the glaze and place them on a cooling rack with a baking sheet underneath to catch any drips from the glaze. Allow the glaze to set for 1 hour before serving.

General Tip: I love to keep my doughnut holes in the refrigerator. They taste refreshing with every bite as the glaze sets and stays crisp when chilled.

Chocolate Chip Muffins

Dairy-Free Option, Refined Sugar–Free
Prep Time: 15 minutes / Bake Time: 18 minutes

There are few things better than having your favorite cookie for breakfast in muffin form. That is exactly what these muffins are, swirled with chocolate chips and then baked to a fluffy golden brown. It's the perfect breakfast for families who are on-the-go in the morning.

Makes **12 muffins**

Nonstick cooking spray
½ cup coconut flour
1 teaspoon baking soda
½ teaspoon baking powder
2 tablespoons coconut sugar
¼ teaspoon salt
2 large eggs, room temperature and beaten
1 teaspoon pure vanilla extract
1 tablespoon apple cider vinegar
1 tablespoon unsalted butter, softened
½ cup vanilla almond milk, room temperature
⅓ cup honey
⅓ cup coconut oil, melted
⅔ cup chocolate chips

1. Preheat the oven to 350°F. Line a 24-cup mini muffin tin with cupcake liners or spray with cooking spray. Set aside.

2. In a medium mixing bowl, combine the flour, baking soda, baking powder, sugar, and salt.

3. In a large mixing bowl, combine the eggs, vanilla, vinegar, butter, almond milk, honey, and oil.

4. Slowly add the dry ingredients to the bowl with the wet ingredients. Using a hand or stand mixer, mix until well combined. Allow the dough to set and thicken for 5 minutes.

5. Fold in the chocolate chips and fill each mini muffin cup three-quarters full with the batter.

6. Bake for 14 to 18 minutes, or until the edges are golden brown and a toothpick inserted into the center of a muffin comes out clean.

7. Allow the muffins to cool slightly before taking them out of the pan. Allow them to continue to cool on a cooling rack before serving.

Substitution Tip: Make this recipe dairy-free by substituting almond butter for the butter and using dairy-free chocolate chips.

Rosemary-Goat Cheese Egg Muffins

Refined Sugar–Free
Prep Time: 10 minutes / **Bake Time:** 17 minutes

These egg muffins are fluffy, soft, and jam-packed with protein and flavor. You won't be able to decide what you like more: the baked egg or the fluffy muffin. Try mixing the flavors up by adding herbs and spices such as thyme, onion powder, garlic powder, Italian seasoning, fennel, or basil.

Makes 12 muffins

Nonstick cooking spray
¼ cup Grain-Free Biscuit Mix (page 16)
5 large eggs, beaten
1½ tablespoons milk
¼ teaspoon freshly ground black pepper
¼ teaspoon garlic salt
2 ounces goat cheese, crumbled
1 handful baby spinach, chopped
6 teaspoons chopped fresh rosemary
Paprika, for sprinkling

1. Preheat the oven to 375°F. Spray a 12-cup muffin tin with cooking spray. Set aside.

2. Mix the biscuit mix, eggs, milk, pepper, and garlic salt in a mixing bowl and set aside.

3. Divide the goat cheese, spinach, and rosemary evenly among the prepared muffin cups.

4. Pour the egg mixture into each muffin cup, filling it halfway. Sprinkle with paprika, then bake for 15 to 17 minutes or until the eggs are fully cooked and the edges of the muffins are a nice golden brown.

5. Remove the muffins from the oven and allow them to cool for 1 to 2 minutes. Run a knife around the edges of each egg muffin before serving.

Ingredient Tip: You can use any meat or veggies that you have on hand for this dish. Try sausage, bacon, ham, broccoli, kale, sweet potato, or bell pepper.

Southern Sausage Kolaches

Refined Sugar–Free
Prep Time: 25 minutes / **Rise Time:** 1 hour / **Bake Time:** 17 minutes

Growing up in Texas, my younger brother and I were introduced to sausage kolaches at an early age. Sausage kolaches are supposed to have originated in Texas and are now a Southern breakfast staple. The sausages are cooked and then wrapped in a warm, soft dough that is lightly seasoned with garlic. To truly make a Southern classic, use a spicy sausage.

Makes 10 kolaches

⅔ cup milk

¼ cup honey

1 (0.25-ounce) package instant yeast

2 large eggs, room temperature and beaten

6 tablespoons (¾ stick) unsalted butter, melted

1 teaspoon garlic salt

4 cups Grain-Free Biscuit Mix (page 16)

2 teaspoons xanthan gum

Olive oil, for coating

5 (hot-dog-size) sausages

Nonstick cooking spray

1. Heat the milk in the microwave to around 110°F, about 30 seconds. You should be able to put your finger in the milk for a few seconds without it being too hot.

2. In a medium mixing bowl, stir the heated milk, honey, and yeast together until thoroughly mixed. Set aside and allow to bloom for 10 minutes.

3. Add the eggs, butter, and garlic salt. Stir to combine. Then, add the biscuit mix and xanthan gum and stir for 2 to 3 minutes until a smooth dough forms.

4. Coat the dough ball in oil and cover the mixing bowl with a clean kitchen towel. Allow to rise for 1 hour in a warm location.

5. While the dough is rising, cut the sausages in half lengthwise. Cook according to the package instructions.

6. Once the dough has risen for 1 hour, preheat the oven to 400°F, then spray a baking sheet with cooking spray.

7. Divide the dough into 10 equal-size pieces. Press each dough ball into a rectangle ½ inch thick, place one of the cooked sausage halves in the center, then wrap the extra dough around the sausage, pinching the dough closed at the seam. Repeat these steps with the rest of the dough and sausages. Place the dough-covered sausages seam-side down on the baking sheet.

8. Bake the kolaches for 15 to 17 minutes or until the tops and edges of each are golden brown. Remove them from the oven and allow them to cool to room temperature before serving.

Substitution Tip: Feel free to substitute pure maple syrup for the honey. It's delicious in this recipe.

CHAPTER SEVEN

PANCAKES, CREPES, AND WAFFLES

Whether you prefer breakfast for breakfast, or breakfast for dinner, the following recipes are so tasty, they will become part of your meal rotation in no time. Not only are they fast and easy to make, they're even easier and quicker to devour. Choose sweet or savory. You can't go wrong, whether it's morning, noon, or night.

Classic Pancakes

Refined Sugar–Free
Prep Time: 5 minutes / Cook Time: 1 hour

Pancakes, flapjacks, breakfast cakes—whatever you call them, we can all agree that a pancake needs to be golden, soft, fluffy, and perfectly round. Add your favorite chocolate chips, nuts, berries, or fruit pieces to make these quick and easy pancakes completely customizable. They're also great to make ahead. Refrigerate and quickly microwave a pancake for 10 to 15 seconds to restore it to its former glory.

Makes 12 pancakes

3 tablespoons coconut oil
4 large eggs
¼ cup milk or cream
½ cup Grain-Free Biscuit Mix (page 16)

1. In a large skillet over low heat, melt the oil, then pour it into a large mixing bowl, leaving a few beads of oil in the skillet.

2. Add the eggs and milk to the bowl, then whisk until fully incorporated. Add the biscuit mix and stir until smooth.

3. Turn the heat on the skillet to medium-low, then pour the batter into the pan, 2 tablespoons at a time. Let each pancake cook for 2 to 3 minutes on one side until golden brown. Flip the pancake and cook until the same color is achieved. Repeat until you've used all the batter.

4. Using a spatula, remove each pancake from the skillet and serve warm.

General Tip: Keep cooked pancakes warm by stacking them on one another and wrapping them in a clean, warm kitchen towel on a plate in the microwave. If you need your pancakes warmed up a bit, microwave them on high for 15-second increments until the desired temperature is achieved.

Confetti Crepes

Refined Sugar–Free
Prep Time: 15 minutes / Cook Time: 28 minutes

Sprinkles make everything more fun, from cupcakes to ice cream sundaes to soft, rolled crepes. Many times, grain-free crepes are extremely crumbly and break apart. However, this recipe creates a crepe that not only looks adorable but also rolls up easily. Soft and doughy, they won't crack or break when manipulated, and on top of it all, they taste like fun.

Makes **4 crepes**

1 large egg
1 large egg white
1 cup milk
1 cup Grain-Free Biscuit Mix (page 16)
2 teaspoons monk fruit baking sugar
1 tablespoon pure vanilla extract
Butter-flavored nonstick cooking spray
Rainbow sprinkles, for topping

1. In a medium mixing bowl, beat the egg and egg white together. Whisk in the milk. Then, stir in the biscuit mix, sugar, and vanilla. Allow to rest for 5 to 10 minutes.

2. Heat a medium nonstick skillet over low heat and coat with butter-flavored cooking spray. Add one-quarter of the crepe batter to the hot skillet. Immediately lift the skillet and swirl the batter around, spreading it out into a thin, even layer. Add your desired amount of sprinkles. Cook for 4 to 7 minutes or until the edges are golden brown and the center of the crepe has set. Transfer the crepe to a plate and repeat for the remaining three crepes.

3. Allow the crepes to cool before serving.

Variation Tip: These confetti crepes are fantastic paired with whipped cream and chocolate or caramel sauce, or sprinkled with monk fruit powdered sugar.

Mini Banana Pancakes

Dairy-Free, Freezable, Refined Sugar–Free
Prep Time: 5 minutes / Cook Time: 40 minutes

These mini pancakes combine the deliciousness of warm banana with the softness of fluffy coconut flour sprinkled with a pinch of cinnamon. They're the perfect small breakfast to warm you up and start your day. Add a few chocolate chips to take them to the next level.

Makes **8 pancakes**

2 large eggs
2 tablespoons coconut flour
¼ teaspoon baking powder
Pinch ground cinnamon
1 banana, mashed
Coconut oil or nonstick cooking spray

1. In a small bowl, whisk together the eggs, coconut flour, baking powder, and cinnamon.

2. Add the mashed banana to the mixture and stir well to combine.

3. Heat a small nonstick skillet over medium heat and coat with coconut oil. Drop a 2-tablespoon scoop of batter onto the skillet and cook until the edges of the pancake become easy to lift from the skillet with a spatula, 2 to 3 minutes. Flip and cook for another 1 to 2 minutes or until the pancake is cooked through. Repeat until all the batter is used.

Baking Tip: Keep these pancakes small in diameter. Making them larger than described in the recipe can lead to the pancake breaking when you flip it over.

Egg Waffles

Nut-Free, Refined Sugar–Free
Prep Time: 5 minutes / Cook Time: 16 minutes

This is one of my family's favorite breakfasts that I make for them. It's also one of my favorites because it contains only two main ingredients and bakes in a few minutes with almost no effort. I love to add garlic powder and Italian seasoning to the batter for some extra flair, but season them as you wish.

Makes **4 waffles**

4 large eggs, beaten
2 cups shredded sharp
  Cheddar cheese
1 teaspoon garlic
  powder (optional)
1 teaspoon Italian
  seasoning (optional)

1. Heat your waffle maker to low-medium heat.

2. In a medium mixing bowl, combine the eggs and cheese until thoroughly mixed.

3. Add the garlic powder and Italian seasoning, if using.

4. Add a quarter of the waffle batter to the heated waffle maker. Cook the batter until no more steam escapes the waffle maker and the edges of the waffle are turning golden brown, 3 to 4 minutes. Repeat for the remaining three waffles.

Baking Tip: Waffle makers all work a little differently. While cooking your first waffle, watch it closely for signs that the waffle is done and take note of the exact time the first one is done. Follow suit with the rest of your batter.

Dutch Baby

Nut-Free, Refined Sugar–Free
Prep Time: 5 minutes / Bake Time: 15 minutes

A Dutch baby is similar to a pancake in shape and diameter, but it's much thicker. This soft, round baked goody uses cheese to help hold it all together. The Swiss cheese keeps the warm center of the Dutch baby gooey and doughy. I love to use whatever seasonal veggies I have available in this pancake, and the Parmesan cheese is the ideal finishing touch.

Serves 4

3 large eggs
¾ cup heavy (whipping) cream
1½ cups tapioca flour
1 teaspoon xanthan gum
1 cup shredded Swiss cheese
4 tablespoons (½ stick) salted butter
1 cup chopped fresh vegetables of choice
¼ cup freshly grated Parmesan cheese, divided
Pinch black pepper

1. Preheat the oven to 425°F.

2. Whisk together the eggs, heavy cream, tapioca flour, xanthan gum, and Swiss cheese.

3. In a 10-inch oven-safe skillet, melt the butter on the stovetop. Carefully pour the dough mixture over the melted butter in the skillet.

4. Sprinkle the chopped vegetables on top of the pancake dough and sprinkle with half of the Parmesan cheese. Bake for 12 to 15 minutes or until the Dutch baby becomes golden brown and bubbly around the edges.

5. Sprinkle black pepper and the remaining Parmesan cheese on top and serve warm in slices.

Baking Tip: You should take out your Dutch baby when the edges become golden brown and bubbly, yet the center is still moist and doughy. The center will look much less done than the outside edges. Once removed from the oven to cool, the center area of the Dutch baby will set.

Perfect Golden Waffles

Dairy-Free Option, Refined Sugar–Free
Prep Time: 15 minutes / Cook Time: 12 to 16 minutes

I changed this recipe around 20 times before getting it perfect. The smooth batter transforms into perfectly indented, soft, fluffy waffles. I like to enjoy these waffles for breakfast, drizzled with pure maple syrup or honey, but they're also incredible when used as the outer layers of an ice cream sandwich or topped with whipped cream, berries, and chocolate sauce.

Makes 3 or 4 waffles

6 large eggs, beaten
4 tablespoons (½ stick) unsalted butter, melted
3 tablespoons coconut flour
⅓ cup Grain-Free Biscuit Mix (page 16)
1 tablespoon light brown coconut sugar

1. Heat your waffle maker to medium heat.

2. In a medium mixing bowl, combine the eggs and butter until just combined.

3. Add the coconut flour, biscuit mix, and sugar. With a hand mixer on medium speed, mix well. Let the mixture sit for 10 minutes.

4. Add the batter to the heated waffle maker in the amount specified by the waffle maker instructions. I fill mine with ½ cup of batter to make 3 large waffles.

5. Cook the batter until no more steam is escaping the waffle maker and the edges of the waffle are turning golden brown, 3 to 4 minutes. Serve warm.

Substitution Tip: Make this recipe dairy-free by substituting dairy-free butter for the butter and using coconut milk powder in the Grain-Free Biscuit Mix (page 16) instead of milk powder.

Soft Cheese Crepes

Refined Sugar–Free
Prep Time: 20 minutes / **Cook Time:** 50 minutes

These soft and doughy crepes are both sweet and savory. The coconut flour and monk fruit sugar, combined with the Cheddar cheese, make every bite of these crepes more and more irresistible. Roll them up and eat them plain like I do, pair them with spicy entrees, or stuff them with a sweet cream cheese.

Makes 10 crepes

2 cups milk or cream
1 cup shredded sharp
   Cheddar cheese
2 large eggs, room
   temperature and
   beaten
1½ cups Grain-Free
   Biscuit Mix (page 16)
1 tablespoon xanthan
   gum
1 tablespoon monk fruit
   baking sugar
½ teaspoon salt
¼ teaspoon cracked
   black pepper
1½ tablespoons olive oil
Nonstick cooking spray

1. Put the milk in a medium saucepan and heat over medium heat until simmering. Once simmering, turn off the heat and add the cheese, stirring until all the cheese is melted. Set aside and allow the mixture to cool to room temperature, 10 to 15 minutes.

2. Add the eggs and stir for 1 to 2 more minutes until smooth. Add the biscuit mix, xanthan gum, sugar, salt, and pepper. Stir for another 1 to 2 minutes until smooth. Lastly, stir in the oil until well combined.

3. Heat a medium nonstick skillet over low heat and spray it with cooking spray. Add ⅓ cup of batter to the heated skillet. Immediately swirl the skillet around to disperse the batter into an even, thin layer. Cook for 2 to 3 minutes or until the bottom of the crepe is turning golden brown and the edges are starting to pull away from the skillet. Carefully flip the crepe over using a spatula and cook for another 1 to 2 minutes or until the other side turns golden brown. Transfer the crepe to a large plate. Repeat with the rest of the batter.

4. Once cooled slightly, roll each crepe or leave it flat, depending on your serving preference.

German Pancake

Dairy-Free Option, Refined Sugar–Free
Prep Time: 10 minutes / Bake Time: 15 minutes

When I think of German baked goods, I always go straight for the sweet gooeyness of brown sugar, cinnamon, and baked apples. This recipe has all those delectable flavors and more. It's thick and doughy, with billowy edges from the skillet. Tear off soft pieces of this warm pancake topped with tender apple slices or cut it into slices like a pie. And if you haven't guessed yet, it is even better with a sprinkle of monk fruit powdered sugar on top!

Serves 4

3 large eggs
¾ cup heavy (whipping) cream
1 cup tapioca flour
½ cup arrowroot flour
½ cup coconut flour
1 teaspoon xanthan gum
½ cup light brown coconut sugar
½ teaspoon ground cinnamon
4 tablespoons (½ stick) salted butter
1 tart apple, cored and sliced
Monk fruit powdered sugar, for topping

1. Preheat the oven to 425°F.

2. In a medium bowl, whisk together the eggs, heavy cream, tapioca flour, arrowroot flour, coconut flour, and xanthan gum. In a small bowl, mix the coconut sugar and cinnamon together.

3. Melt the butter in a 10-inch oven-safe skillet over medium heat. Carefully pour the dough mixture over the melted butter in the skillet.

4. Sprinkle the apple slices on top of the pancake dough and sprinkle with half of the cinnamon-sugar mixture. Bake for 12 to 15 minutes or until the pancake becomes golden brown and bubbly around the edges.

5. Sprinkle the remaining cinnamon-sugar on top of the pancake as well as a sprinkle of powdered sugar and serve warm.

Substitution Tip: To make this recipe dairy-free, replace the heavy cream with the liquid portion of full-fat coconut milk and the butter with dairy-free butter.

CHAPTER EIGHT

PIES AND TARTS

Pies are delectable no matter what time of year it is. There's nothing better in the fall than a warm pie or cobbler coming out of a hot oven. There's also nothing better in the summer than biting into a light and fresh strawberry galette. The recipes in this chapter that use fruit as a staple ingredient can be interchanged with other comparable fruits for pies and tarts to your liking.

Simple Pie Crust

Egg-Free, Freezable, Nut-Free
Prep Time: 10 minutes / **Chill Time:** 2 hours

This pie crust is easy to make with just a few simple ingredients. It's also very hard to mess up and turns out perfectly golden and deliciously soft. You can freeze or store this crust for months at a time so you always have it on hand.

Makes 2 pie crusts

3 cups store-bought all-purpose gluten-free flour blend

2 tablespoons granulated sugar

¾ teaspoon salt

1 cup (2 sticks) plus 5 tablespoons butter, cubed and frozen

½ cup cold water with added ice

Baking Tip: You can use this pie crust according to your pie recipe's instructions, whether you need to parbake (partially bake the crust before adding filling to the pie) or not. Be sure to carefully read and follow the specific recipe to know if you need to parbake.

1. Mix the flour, sugar, and salt in a stand mixer with the paddle attachment.

2. With the mixer on low speed, drop a few pieces of the frozen butter at a time into the flour mixture. Wait until the butter is coated in flour before you add a few more pieces. Do this until all the butter has been added. The mixture will be lumpy and not homogeneous.

3. Remove the ice from the cold water and pour out any excess water that may have been added by the melting ice. While the mixer is still on low speed, slowly pour the cold water, a little at a time, into the dough mixture. Continue with the mixer on low speed until the water is fully incorporated and a thick dough forms. It should stick to the paddle attachment.

4. Divide the dough into two large balls and tightly wrap each in plastic wrap. Then, wrap each dough ball in a second piece of plastic wrap or store in a food-safe plastic storage bag.

5. Chill the dough in the refrigerator for 1½ to 2 hours. After chilling, the dough can be used immediately or stored in the freezer for 3 to 4 months. If freezing, thaw the frozen dough in the refrigerator for 24 hours when ready to use.

Blackberry Crumble

Freezable, Refined Sugar–Free
Prep Time: 10 minutes / Bake Time: 35 minutes

I've been making this recipe for almost two decades now. Every time I do, I'm surprised by the comfort, warmth, and decadence of every bite.

Serves 8

FOR THE FRUIT FILLING
Nonstick cooking spray
4 cups fresh blackberries
⅓ cup monk fruit baking sugar
⅓ cup light brown coconut sugar
3 tablespoons arrowroot starch
1 tablespoon freshly squeezed lemon juice
1 teaspoon pure vanilla extract
Pinch salt

FOR THE CRUMBLE TOPPING
¾ cup finely chopped pecans
½ cup almond flour
⅓ cup unsalted butter, melted
⅓ cup light brown coconut sugar
½ teaspoon ground cinnamon

1. Preheat the oven to 350°F. Spray a 9-by-9-inch baking dish with cooking spray and set aside.

2. To make the fruit filling, in a large mixing bowl, combine the blackberries, monk fruit sugar, coconut sugar, arrowroot starch, lemon juice, vanilla, and salt and mix well.

3. To make the crumble topping, in a second mixing bowl, combine the pecans, almond flour, butter, coconut sugar, and cinnamon. Mix well.

4. Transfer the fruit filling to the prepared baking dish. Sprinkle the crumble topping on top and spread into an even layer. Bake for 30 to 35 minutes, or until the blackberry filling is bubbling along the sides and the crumble is a golden brown around the edges.

5. Allow the blackberry crumble to cool before serving.

Ingredient Tip: Use your favorite seasonal fruit in this recipe for a change. I like strawberries and raspberries as well. Try topping the crumble with ice cream and a drizzle of pure maple syrup or honey!

Apple Cobbler

Freezable, Refined Sugar–Free
Prep Time: 20 minutes / Cook Time: 50 minutes

This apple cobbler uses fresh apples that are warmed beneath a layer of warm and gooey cookie-like batter. All the nooks and crannies between the apples fill with a delicious, sweet drizzle. There is no better comfort than taking this cobbler out of the oven, its sweet aromas swirling.

Serves 8

Nonstick cooking spray

4 cups sliced apples

2 tablespoons arrowroot starch

1 cup monk fruit baking sugar, divided

1½ cups Sweet Grain-Free Flour Blend (page 14)

½ cup packed light brown coconut sugar

¼ teaspoon salt

2 teaspoons baking powder

6 tablespoons (¾ stick) cold unsalted butter, cubed

¾ cup milk

1. Preheat the oven to 325°F, then spray a 9-by-9-inch baking pan with cooking spray. Set aside.

2. In a large mixing bowl, combine the sliced apples, arrowroot starch, and ½ cup of monk fruit sugar.

3. In a second bowl, combine the flour blend, the remaining ½ cup of monk fruit sugar, the coconut sugar, salt, and baking powder. Then, add the cubed cold butter and mix until the mixture reaches a crumbly consistency. Stir in the milk to create a dough.

4. Spread the apple mixture into the greased pan. Drop the dough by large spoonfuls on top of the fruit mix for an even layer of batter.

5. Bake for 40 to 50 minutes or until the cobbler is golden on top and fruit juice is bubbling along the sides of the pan.

6. Let the cobbler sit for 5 minutes to set, then serve while still warm.

Baking Tip: If your cobbler is becoming too browned on top, cover it with aluminum foil for the last 20 minutes of baking.

Variation Tip: I like to sprinkle monk fruit powdered sugar and chopped pecans on top of the batter just before it goes into the oven for a little bit of a sweet crunch.

Sweet Cherry Galette

Freezable, Refined Sugar–Free
Prep Time: 35 minutes / **Bake Time:** 26 minutes

There is just something about warm, juicy cherries smothered in sweet sauce inside a tender crust. This galette is as easy to put together as it is to devour.

Serves 8

FOR THE FRUIT FILLING
3½ cups cherries, pitted
2 tablespoons monk fruit baking sugar
1 tablespoon arrowroot starch
1 teaspoon freshly squeezed lemon juice
1 teaspoon pure vanilla extract

FOR THE CRUST
1 Simple Pie Crust (page 86)
1 large egg, beaten
2 tablespoons monk fruit baking sugar

FOR THE LEMON GLAZE
¾ cup monk fruit powdered sugar
2 to 3 tablespoons milk
½ teaspoon freshly squeezed lemon juice

1. Preheat the oven to 400°F.

2. To make the fruit filling, in a large mixing bowl, combine the cherries, baking sugar, arrowroot starch, lemon juice, and vanilla and mix well.

3. To prepare the crust, lay out a sheet of parchment paper on your work surface. Roll the chilled pie crust dough into a 12-inch circle, then transfer the parchment and dough to a baking sheet.

4. Spoon the fruit filling onto the center of the dough. Flip up the outer edges of the dough together to form a bowl with the fruit in the center.

5. Brush the outside edges of the dough with the beaten egg and sprinkle with the baking sugar.

6. Bake for 22 to 26 minutes or until the edges of the crust are golden brown and the fruit juices are bubbling.

7. Remove the galette from the oven and allow it to cool.

8. For the lemon glaze, combine the powdered sugar, milk, and lemon juice in a small bowl. Drizzle the glaze over the cooled galette and serve.

Ingredient Tip: The amount of milk in the lemon glaze depends on how thick you like the icing. Less milk yields a thicker icing and more milk yields a thinner one.

Strawberry Galette

Freezable, Refined Sugar–Free
Prep Time: 20 minutes / Chill Time: 30 minutes / Bake Time: 26 minutes

This strawberry galette combines a bowl-shaped crisp crust, perfectly golden on top, with a flavorful center. The strawberry filling mixes the berries with sugar, vanilla, and lemon juice for a sweet yet fresh flavor. To top it all off, a light citrus icing drizzle is added to the top before serving.

Serves 8

FOR THE CRUST
1¾ cups Sweet Grain-Free Flour Blend (page 14)
5 tablespoons monk fruit baking sugar, divided
½ teaspoon salt
8 tablespoons (1 stick) very cold unsalted butter, cubed
6 tablespoons ice water
1 large egg, beaten

1. Preheat the oven to 400°F.

TO MAKE THE CRUST

2. Combine the flour blend, 3 tablespoons of baking sugar, salt, butter, and ice water in a large mixing bowl. Mix together until well combined. Roll the dough into a ball, flatten into a disk, wrap in plastic wrap, and chill in the refrigerator for 20 to 30 minutes while the oven heats up.

TO MAKE THE FRUIT FILLING

3. While the dough chills, put the strawberries, baking sugar, arrowroot starch, lemon juice, and vanilla in a large mixing bowl. Mix well.

4. Once the dough has chilled, lay out a sheet of parchment paper on your work surface and roll the dough into a 12-inch circle. Transfer the parchment and dough to a baking sheet.

5. Spoon the fruit filling onto the center of the dough. Flip up the outer edges of the dough to form a bowl with the fruit in the center.

4 cups sliced
   strawberries

2 tablespoons monk
   fruit baking sugar

1 tablespoon arrowroot
   starch

1 teaspoon freshly
   squeezed lemon juice

1 teaspoon pure vanilla
   extract

FOR THE CITRUS GLAZE

¾ cup monk fruit
   powdered sugar

2 to 3 tablespoons milk

½ teaspoon freshly
   squeezed lemon or
   lime juice

6. Brush the outside edges of the dough with the beaten egg and sprinkle with the remaining 2 tablespoons of baking sugar. Bake for 22 to 26 minutes or until the edges of the crust are golden brown and the fruit juices are bubbling.

7. Remove the galette from the oven and allow it to cool.

TO MAKE THE CITRUS GLAZE

8. In a small mixing bowl, mix the powdered sugar, milk, and lemon juice until well combined. Drizzle the glaze over the cooled galette.

Variation Tip: The amount of milk in the citrus glaze depends on how thick you like the icing. For a thicker citrus glaze, use less milk. For a thinner glaze, use more.

Peach Pie

Egg-Free, Freezable, Refined Sugar–Free
Prep Time: 20 minutes / Bake Time: 45 minutes

Summers here in Georgia are full of fresh peaches, sometimes to the point where you don't know what to do with them all! My favorite way to eat peaches, besides fresh, is to bake them in a simple peach pie. This recipe incorporates my Simple Pie Crust (page 86) and slices of sweet, fresh peaches. Take this pie out of the oven, give it just enough time to cool and set, then serve it with a huge dollop of vanilla ice cream.

Serves 8

1 Simple Pie Crust
  (page 86)
4 to 5 peaches, peeled,
  pitted, and cubed
¼ cup arrowroot starch
¼ cup tapioca flour
¾ cup (150g) monk fruit
  baking sugar
¼ cup light brown
  coconut sugar
½ teaspoon cinnamon
½ teaspoon salt

1. Preheat the oven to 450°F.

2. Roll out the chilled pie crust and carefully place it in a 9-inch pie pan. Keep the pie crust refrigerated while you prepare the filling.

3. In a large mixing bowl, combine the peaches, arrowroot starch, tapioca flour, monk fruit sugar, coconut sugar, cinnamon, and salt. Mix well.

4. Remove the pie crust from the refrigerator and pour the filling into the crust.

5. Place the pie on a rimmed baking sheet and bake for 20 minutes. Remove the pie from the oven, cover it with aluminum foil, and bake for another 25 minutes or until the edge turns a warm, golden brown and the fruit juices are bubbling around the edges.

6. Remove the pie from the oven and cool to room temperature before slicing.

Baking Tip: The baking time will depend on how ripe your peaches are. The riper the peaches, the less time your pie will need to bake in the oven to become tender.

Pumpkin Pie

Freezable, Refined Sugar–Free
Prep Time: 10 minutes / **Cook Time:** 55 minutes

There is nothing more comforting in the fall than a piece of homemade pumpkin pie. To me, a pumpkin pie needs a smooth, thick pumpkin center and a warm golden crust. My Simple Pie Crust (page 86) is used in this recipe, so you get a tender, doughy crust in every bite. I like to top my slice of pie with homemade whipped cream or vanilla bean ice cream and a sprinkle of chopped nuts.

Serves 8

1 Simple Pie Crust (page 86)
¾ cup monk fruit baking sugar
1 teaspoon ground cinnamon
¾ teaspoon ground nutmeg
½ teaspoon salt
⅛ teaspoon ground cloves
2 large eggs, beaten
1 (15-ounce) can pumpkin puree
1 (12-ounce) can unsweetened evaporated milk

1. Preheat the oven to 425°F. Roll the chilled pie crust into a 9-inch circle and carefully transfer it to a 9-inch pie pan. Keep the crust in the refrigerator while you prepare the filling.

2. Combine the sugar, cinnamon, nutmeg, salt, and cloves in a large mixing bowl and stir until well combined.

3. Mix the eggs into the dry ingredients, followed by the pumpkin puree, and stir until combined. Add the evaporated milk, stirring until well combined.

4. Pour the pumpkin pie filling into the pie crust, then bake for 15 minutes on the center rack. Lower the oven temperate to 350°F and remove the pie. Place aluminum foil over the top and sides of the pie, then return it to the oven. Bake for another 35 to 40 minutes or until a toothpick inserted into the center of the pie comes out clean.

5. Remove the pie from the oven and allow it to cool to room temperature before serving.

Deep Chocolate Torte

Freezable, Nut-Free, Refined Sugar–Free
Prep Time: 20 minutes / Cook Time: 30 minutes / Set Time: 1 hour

If you're looking for a decadent chocolate dessert for your next party, then look no further. This torte has a dense chocolate cake–like base smothered in a homemade chocolate ganache that leaves a smooth, shiny coating. Fresh berries give a hint of tartness to cut the richness of all the chocolate.

Serves 8

Nonstick cooking spray
1¼ cups (2½ sticks) salted butter, divided
14 ounces dark chocolate chips, divided
1½ cups monk fruit powdered sugar
6 large eggs
1 cup unsweetened cocoa powder
1½ cups berries of choice, washed

Ingredient Tip: The chocolate ganache will harden slightly, so be sure to place the berries on while it's still wet. This will let the berries settle into the torte for a perfect chocolate dessert.

1. Preheat the oven to 375°F, then spray an oven-safe 9-inch pie pan with cooking spray. Set aside.

2. Place a medium saucepan inside a large saucepan. Fill the large saucepan two-thirds of the way with boiling water. Inside the medium saucepan, combine 1 cup (2 sticks) of butter and 8 ounces of chocolate chips. Stir until melted.

3. Remove the medium saucepan from the heat and add the powdered sugar, eggs, and cocoa powder, stirring until well combined.

4. Pour the batter into the prepared pie pan and bake for 22 to 24 minutes or cooked but still jiggly. Let cool for 15 minutes.

5. Place a serving platter on top of the pie pan, then carefully flip them over so the torte lands upright on the platter.

6. In a small bowl, combine the remaining 4 tablespoons (½ stick) of butter and 6 ounces of chocolate chips. Microwave on high for 30-second increments, stirring in between, until melted and combined. Pour the chocolate sauce on top of the cooled torte and spread it out evenly. Place your berries on top and allow to set for 1 hour before serving.

Chocolate Mousse Pie

Egg-Free, Freezable, Refined Sugar–Free
Prep Time: 15 minutes / **Chill Time:** 2 hours / **Cook Time:** 30 minutes

What could be better than decadent fluffy chocolate atop a soft doughy crust? This chocolate mousse is made by whipping melted chocolate and whipping cream into light, airy perfection before being poured into a freshly baked pie crust.

Serves 6 to 8

8 ounces dark baking chocolate, coarsely chopped

2 cups heavy (whipping) cream, divided

2 tablespoons monk fruit powdered sugar

2 teaspoons pure vanilla extract

1 Simple Pie Crust (page 86)

Variation Tip: Sprinkle the top of the pie with a generous amount of monk fruit powdered sugar for an extra wow factor and sweetness.

1. Put the chopped chocolate in a large heat-safe mixing bowl. Pour 1 cup of cream into a small saucepan. Heat over medium heat until it starts to simmer, then pour it over the chocolate. Stir the mixture until the chocolate has melted entirely.

2. Add the powdered sugar and vanilla to the mixture. Stir continuously while adding the remaining 1 cup of cream until the mixture is smooth. Cover the bowl and place it in the refrigerator to chill for 1 to 2 hours.

3. While the mousse is chilling, preheat the oven to 350°F. Roll the pie crust out into a 9-inch circle and carefully transfer it to a 9-inch pie pan. Bake for 20 to 25 minutes or until the top turns a soft golden brown. Remove the pie crust from the oven and let it cool to room temperature.

4. Once the crust is cooled, remove the chilled mousse from the refrigerator and whip it using a stand mixer on medium speed until stiff peaks form, 1 to 2 minutes.

5. Pour the chocolate mousse into the cooled pie crust and spread into an even layer. Serve immediately.

SAVORY BAKES

This is one of my favorite chapters in this entire book—savory baked snacks. The recipes in this chapter combine doughy bites with garlic, basil, thyme, and yummy cheeses. There are also crisp crackers and chips with perfect golden edges and savory spices. Many of these recipes are great with sauces that can be used as dips or drizzles, such as marinara sauce, pesto, or spiced oil and vinegar.

Easy Pita Chips

Egg-Free, Freezable, Nut-Free, Refined Sugar–Free
Prep Time: 20 minutes / Chill Time: 15 minutes / Rise Time: 1½ hours
Cook Time: 10 minutes

Sometimes I need a snack or appetizer for a get-together that is extra easy so I can focus on other things. Enter this pita chip recipe. It is simple to put together and produces my all-time favorite homemade pita chip. Once cut into triangles, they're perfect for dipping into hummus. Plus, they're easy to freeze so you can enjoy them later.

Serves 8

¾ cup warm (115°F) water

1 (0.25-ounce) package instant yeast

2 teaspoons honey

1½ cups cassava flour, plus more for dusting

½ cup tapioca flour

¾ teaspoon baking powder

½ teaspoon salt

¼ cup plain yogurt

1 tablespoon olive oil, plus more for greasing and cooking

1 teaspoon apple cider vinegar

1. In a small bowl, combine the warm water, yeast, and honey. Let the mixture rest for 5 to 10 minutes or until fizzy on top.

2. In a stand mixer, mix the cassava flour, tapioca flour, baking powder, and salt together. Then, add the yeast mixture and mix until combined.

3. Add the yogurt, oil, and vinegar and mix until well combined.

4. Using the dough hook attachment or your hands, knead the dough for 1 to 2 minutes.

5. Place the dough in an oiled bowl and cover with a clean kitchen towel. Place the bowl in a warm location and allow the dough to rise for 1½ hours or until the dough has doubled in size.

6. Once the dough has risen, place it in the refrigerator to chill for 10 to 15 minutes.

7. Flour your hands and counter space, then divide the dough into 4 or 5 equal-size balls. Place each dough ball between two sheets of wax paper and roll them into circles about ¼ inch thick.

8. Drizzle a large nonstick pan with oil and heat over medium-high heat. Place each piece of dough on the heated pan, one at a time, and cook for 30 to 60 seconds or until the bottom starts to turn a deep golden brown and the edges begin to puff up. Using a spatula, carefully flip the pita and cook for an additional 30 to 90 seconds or until the second side looks like the first side. Transfer the cooked pita bread to a cooling rack and let it cool for 3 to 4 minutes. Repeat until all the pitas have been cooked and cooled.

9. Slice the pitas into 6 to 8 small triangles. Allow them to fully cool to room temperature before serving.

Preparation Tip: Use a pizza cutter to quickly and easily cut the pita bread rounds into their ultimate triangle-like shape.

"Everything but the Bagel" Crackers

Egg-Free, Freezable, Refined Sugar–Free
Prep Time: 5 minutes / **Chill Time:** 10 minutes / **Bake Time:** 13 minutes

Everything bagel seasoning is absolutely delicious on most savory baked goods but especially on these cheesy, crispy crackers. The center remains just a little doughy, while the edges harden, making them an excellent base for your favorite dip. But honestly, they're delicious enough to eat all on their own.

Serves 8

1 cup almond flour
1 cup shredded Swiss
  cheese
4½ tablespoons
  unsalted butter,
  softened
Nonstick cooking spray
Coarse sea salt, to taste
3 to 4 tablespoons
  everything bagel
  seasoning

1. In a food processor, combine the flour, cheese, and butter and mix until a dough forms.

2. Wrap the dough ball in plastic wrap and allow it to chill in the refrigerator for 10 minutes.

3. Preheat the oven to 350°F. Lay out a sheet of parchment paper and spray a rolling pin with cooking spray.

4. Working quickly so as to not warm the chilled dough, roll the dough out on the parchment into a rectangle about ¼ inch thick. Cut the dough into 1-inch squares, then transfer the parchment and dough to a baking sheet. Generously sprinkle the dough with the salt and everything bagel seasoning. Bake for 11 to 13 minutes.

5. Remove the crackers from the oven and allow them to cool for 1 to 2 minutes before going over your cut marks with a knife again. Allow them to cool fully so they properly crisp up, then enjoy.

Preparation Tip: To easily cut the crackers before and after baking, use a pizza cutter.

Italian-Style Breadsticks

Dairy-Free, Egg-Free, Freezable, Refined Sugar–Free
Prep Time: 10 minutes / **Bake Time:** 16 minutes

These addictive breadsticks are the perfect accompaniment to any meal. They're soft on the inside and crisp on the outside, with a golden crust and savory Italian herbs. They're dense enough to dunk into marinara or Alfredo sauce and delicious enough to enjoy any time of the day. I may be eating one for breakfast right now!

Serves 10

1 cup almond flour
1½ cups tapioca flour
½ teaspoon baking powder
1 teaspoon salt, plus more for topping
½ cup water, room temperature
2 tablespoons olive oil
10 teaspoons Italian seasoning

1. Preheat the oven to 350°F, then line a large baking sheet with parchment paper. Set aside.

2. In a large mixing bowl, combine the almond flour, tapioca flour, baking powder, and salt. Mix well.

3. Add the water and oil to the dry ingredients and mix thoroughly until the dough is homogeneous.

4. Divide the dough evenly into 10 portions and spoon the dough onto the lined baking sheet into 6-by-2-inch rectangles, about 1 inch thick.

5. Sprinkle each breadstick with 1 teaspoon of Italian seasoning and a pinch of salt.

6. Bake the breadsticks for 14 to 16 minutes or until crispy and golden brown around the edges.

7. Remove from the oven and allow them to cool for 10 minutes before serving.

Crispy Cheese Crackers

Dairy-Free Option, Freezable, Nut-Free, Refined Sugar–Free
Prep Time: 5 minutes / Chill Time: 10 minutes / Bake Time: 15 minutes

One of the things that I missed most on a grain-free diet are those little Cheddar-flavored crispy crackers topped with coarse sprinkles of sea salt. But this cracker is a game-changer, with sharp Cheddar flavor, crisp golden edges, and the added crunch of sea salt. Now I don't miss those grain-full processed cheese crackers at all.

Serves 8

1 cup tapioca flour
1 cup sharp Cheddar
    cheese, shredded
4½ tablespoons
    unsalted butter,
    softened
Nonstick cooking spray
Coarse sea salt, to taste

1. In a food processor, combine the flour, cheese, and butter and process until a dough forms.

2. Wrap the dough in plastic wrap and chill in the refrigerator for 10 minutes.

3. Preheat the oven to 350°F. Lay out a sheet of parchment paper on your work surface and spray a rolling pin with cooking spray.

4. Working quickly so as to not warm the chilled dough, roll it out on the parchment into a rectangle about ¼ inch thick. Cut the dough into 1-inch squares, generously sprinkle with the sea salt, and bake for 13 to 15 minutes.

5. Remove the crackers from the oven and allow them to cool for 1 to 2 minutes before going over your cut marks again with a knife. Allow the crackers to cool completely to crisp up, then enjoy.

Preparation Tip: To easily cut the crackers before and after baking, use a pizza cutter.

Substitution Tip: To make this recipe dairy-free, use dairy-free cheese and dairy-free butter.

Easy Garlic Croutons

Freezable, Refined Sugar–Free
Prep Time: 5 minutes / **Bake Time:** 8 minutes

Every salad and bowl of soup is best when topped with fresh, crispy croutons. This recipe yields my favorite croutons, using my Sandwich Bread (page 28), butter, and garlic salt. Try using cracked pepper, Italian seasoning, thyme, fennel, or paprika to really make these croutons your own.

Serves 12

3 to 4 tablespoons unsalted butter, melted
2 to 3 tablespoons garlic salt
4 (1-inch-thick) slices Sandwich Bread (page 28), cut into 1-inch cubes

1. Turn on the oven broiler.

2. In a medium mixing bowl, combine the butter and garlic salt. Add the bread cubes and toss well to coat, then place them on a nonstick baking sheet.

3. Broil the croutons for 3 to 4 minutes or until their edges and corners start to toast and become golden brown.

4. Flip the croutons over and broil for another 3 to 4 minutes. Remove them from the oven to cool, then serve.

Preparation Tip: Store these croutons in an airtight bag in the freezer for up to 6 months. When ready to use, remove the amount you need from the freezer, then thaw them at room temperature for 1 to 2 hours.

Fluffy Drop Bombs

Dairy-Free Option, Refined Sugar–Free

Prep Time: 20 minutes / Rise Time: 1 hour / Bake Time: 13 minutes

These soft, buttery, grain-free dinner rolls couldn't be any simpler to make. My savory homemade flour blend is mixed with yeast, warm milk, butter, and honey and then spooned into a baking pan to make these perfectly messy melt-in-your-mouth rolls.

Makes 9 rolls

½ cup plus
  2 tablespoons warm
  (115°F) milk
¼ cup honey
1 (0.25-ounce) package
  instant yeast
1¾ cup Savory
  Grain-Free Flour Blend
  (page 15)
½ teaspoon salt
½ teaspoon xanthan
  gum
4 tablespoons (½ stick)
  unsalted butter,
  softened, divided
1 large egg, room
  temperature
½ teaspoon apple cider
  vinegar
Nonstick cooking spray

1. Pour the milk, honey, and yeast into a small bowl and allow to bloom for 10 minutes.

2. While waiting for the yeast, combine the flour blend, salt, and xanthan gum in a large mixing bowl.

3. Make a small hole with your finger in the middle of the flour mixture and pour the yeast mixture into it.

4. Add 2 tablespoons of butter, the egg, and vinegar, and use the dough hook attachment on a stand mixer or your hands to mix until fully combined, about 2 minutes.

5. Spray a 9-by-9-inch or 8-by-8-inch metal or glass baking pan with cooking spray.

6. Using an ice cream scoop sprayed with cooking spray, evenly scoop out and place 9 dough balls in the pan. If you'd like your rolls smoother, dip a spatula in cool water and use it to smooth the tops of the rolls.

7. Cover the pan with a clean kitchen towel and allow the rolls to rise in a warm location for 1 hour.

8. Preheat the oven to 400°F. When the rolls have risen, bake them on the middle rack for 11 to 13 minutes.

9. Melt the remaining 2 tablespoons of butter, then brush the tops of the rolls with the butter before serving.

Substitution Tip: To make these dairy-free, substitute dairy-free butter for the butter and dairy-free milk for the milk.

Pizza Shop Cheese Sticks

Refined Sugar–Free
Prep Time: 15 minutes / **Bake Time:** 12 minutes

Whenever I went to the neighborhood pizza joint as a kid, my family ordered cheese sticks to go with our pizza. As an adult, I wanted to recreate that experience, so I made this recipe. The sticks here are finger-length cuts of pizza dough smothered in mozzarella cheese and Italian spices. They're the perfect tear-and-share appetizer.

Serves 4

Nonstick cooking spray
1¾ cup Savory Grain-Free Flour Blend (page 15)
1 teaspoon garlic powder
½ teaspoon salt
½ teaspoon xanthan gum
1 (0.25-ounce) package instant yeast
½ cup warm (115°F) milk
3 tablespoons unsalted butter, softened
1 large egg, room temperature
½ teaspoon apple cider vinegar
1 tablespoon honey
1 to 2 cups shredded mozzarella cheese
1 to 2 teaspoons Italian seasoning

1. Preheat the oven to 450°F. Spray a large nonstick baking sheet with cooking spray. Set aside.

2. In a large mixing bowl, combine the flour blend, garlic powder, salt, and xanthan gum.

3. Make a small hole with your finger in the middle of the flour mixture and pour the yeast into that hole. Pour the milk over the yeast.

4. Add the butter, egg, vinegar, and honey to the bowl, then use the dough hook attachment on a stand mixer or a wooden spoon to mix until fully combined, about 2 minutes.

5. Spray your hands with cooking spray and place the dough on the baking sheet. Flatten it into a rectangle ½ inch thick.

6. Bake on the middle rack of the oven for 6 minutes. Remove the bread, then sprinkle the shredded cheese and Italian seasoning evenly on top. Bake for another 4 to 6 minutes, or until the cheese is melted and turning a light golden brown around the edges. Enjoy!

Potato Rolls

Refined Sugar–Free
Prep Time: 10 minutes / Bake Time: 11 minutes

These potato rolls bring me right back to the dinner table with my grandmother. She made potato rolls for every family meal, and now you can too. These soft, savory rolls are best served warm from the oven and are easily the first thing on the table to be devoured. Whether you add butter, a fresh homemade jam, or nothing at all, you will definitely be asking for another.

Makes **24 rolls**

Nonstick cooking spray
1 cup Grain-Free Biscuit
 Mix (page 16)
1 cup mashed potatoes
2 large eggs, room
 temperature
1 teaspoon baking
 powder
¼ cup nutritional yeast
 flakes
¾ teaspoon salt

1. Preheat the oven to 425°F. Spray a 24-cup mini muffin tin with cooking spray. Set aside.

2. In a large mixing bowl, mix the biscuit mix, mashed potatoes, eggs, baking powder, nutritional yeast, and salt until well combined.

3. Place ping-pong-ball-size dough balls into each cup of the mini muffin tin. Bake the rolls for 9 to 11 minutes or until the tops start to turn golden brown.

4. Remove the rolls from the oven and allow them to cool for 1 to 2 minutes before moving each roll to a cooling rack to cool fully before enjoying.

Preparation Tip: If you want the tops of your potato rolls to be nice and smooth, spray the back of a spatula or spoon with cooking spray and gently glide the utensil along the top of each roll to smooth out its appearance before placing them in the oven to bake.

Pizza Bites

Freezable, Nut-Free, Refined Sugar–Free
Prep Time: 10 minutes / **Bake Time:** 36 minutes

Pizza bites start off with a garlicky, soft dough that is quickly baked in the oven. Then you top them with pizza sauce, mozzarella cheese, and pepperoni. (You can add other toppings, like chopped vegetables.) A sprinkle of Italian seasoning finishes these simple snacks off and a quick broil makes them perfectly crispy. These are ideal for your next party or after school study session.

Makes 10 pizza bites

Nonstick cooking spray
3 large eggs, separated
3 tablespoons cream cheese
1½ teaspoons garlic powder
½ teaspoon monk fruit baking sugar
¼ teaspoon cream of tartar
⅔ cup pizza sauce
⅔ cup shredded mozzarella cheese
10 thin slices pepperoni

1. Preheat the oven to 300°F. Spray a baking sheet with cooking spray. Set aside.

2. In a medium mixing bowl, mix together the egg yolks, cream cheese, garlic powder, and sugar until smooth.

3. In a small mixing bowl, beat the egg whites and cream of tartar with a stand or hand mixer on high speed until they are fluffy and form stiff peaks.

4. Very carefully fold the egg yolk mixture into the egg whites until mixed, while not breaking down the fluffiness of the egg whites.

5. Scoop the dough into 10 even rounds onto the baking sheet (4 to 5 inches across and ½ to 1 inch thick).

6. Bake the dough on the middle rack for 25 to 35 minutes. Remove the pizza bites from the oven and allow them to cool for 10 minutes on the baking sheet before transferring them to a cooling rack to cool further. Turn on the oven broiler.

7. Spoon 1 tablespoon of pizza sauce on top of each piece of baked dough. Top the pizza sauce with 1 tablespoon of shredded cheese and 1 slice of pepperoni. Place the pizza bites under the broiler for 30 to 90 seconds, depending on how golden you like your cheese.

Baking Tip: The baking time varies quite a bit in this recipe, so watch the pizza bites carefully. Once they become nice and golden brown on top, remove them from the oven immediately.

Measurement Conversions

VOLUME EQUIVALENTS	U.S. STANDARD	U.S. STANDARD (OUNCES)	METRIC (APPROXIMATE)
LIQUID	2 tablespoons	1 fl. oz.	30 mL
	¼ cup	2 fl. oz.	60 mL
	½ cup	4 fl. oz.	120 mL
	1 cup	8 fl. oz.	240 mL
	1½ cups	12 fl. oz.	355 mL
	2 cups or 1 pint	16 fl. oz.	475 mL
	4 cups or 1 quart	32 fl. oz.	1 L
	1 gallon	128 fl. oz.	4 L
DRY	⅛ teaspoon	–	0.5 mL
	¼ teaspoon	–	1 mL
	½ teaspoon	–	2 mL
	¾ teaspoon	–	4 mL
	1 teaspoon	–	5 mL
	1 tablespoon	–	15 mL
	¼ cup	–	59 mL
	⅓ cup	–	79 mL
	½ cup	–	118 mL
	⅔ cup	–	156 mL
	¾ cup	–	177 mL
	1 cup	–	235 mL
	2 cups or 1 pint	–	475 mL
	3 cups	–	700 mL
	4 cups or 1 quart	–	1 L
	½ gallon	–	2 L
	1 gallon	–	4 L

OVEN TEMPERATURES

FAHRENHEIT	CELSIUS (APPROXIMATE)
250°F	120°C
300°F	150°C
325°F	165°C
350°F	180°C
375°F	190°C
400°F	200°C
425°F	220°C
450°F	230°C

WEIGHT EQUIVALENTS

U.S. STANDARD	METRIC (APPROXIMATE)
½ ounce	15 g
1 ounce	30 g
2 ounces	60 g
4 ounces	115 g
8 ounces	225 g
12 ounces	340 g
16 ounces or 1 pound	455 g

Index

Acknowledgments

I would like to thank my family and friends for their incredible support throughout this book publishing process. I only achieved this success because of my loving, encouraging community. Lastly, thank you to everyone who has read a post, shared a photo, cooked a recipe, or trusted me enough that you went out and spent your own hard-earned money on this book. I appreciate you all.

About the Author

Jessica Kirk is a veterinarian in academia by day and a gluten-free recipe adventurer by night. Jessica is the founder of BlessHerHeartYall.com and currently also runs a veterinary-based website, VetExplainsPets.com. She lives outside of Atlanta, Georgia, where she can be found hiking, biking, riding horses, and dabbling in home renovation projects.

CPSIA information can be obtained
at www.ICGtesting.com
Printed in the USA
JSHW020444200422
25078JS00001B/5

9 781638 787006